TOWARD CIVIL SOCIETY
IN THE MIDDLE EAST?

The Middle East and North Africa

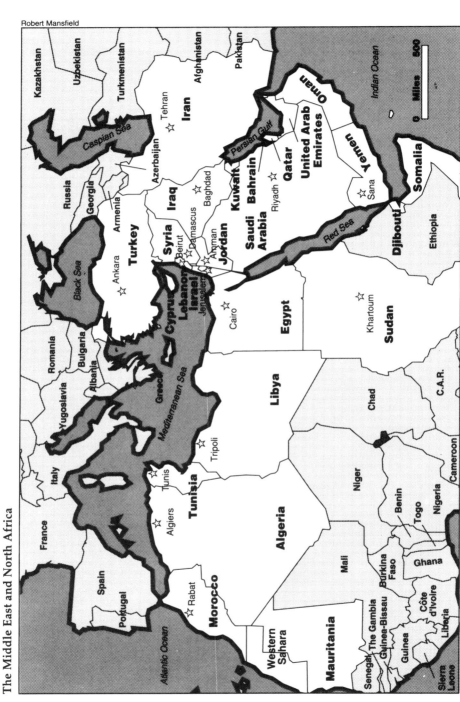

Robert Mansfield

Reprinted courtesy of the Foreign Policy Association, from *Political Tides in the Arab World*, M. Muslih and A. R. Norton, Headline Series No. 296, Summer 1991.

TOWARD CIVIL SOCIETY IN THE MIDDLE EAST?

A PRIMER

EDITED BY

JILLIAN SCHWEDLER

LYNNE
RIENNER
PUBLISHERS

BOULDER
LONDON

Cover photo: from *Quest for Change: Civil Society in the Middle East,*
documentary film produced by Steven Talley and Augustus Richard Norton,
© 1994. Distributed by First Run/Icarus Films, New York, and Lynne Rienner Publishers.

Published in the United States of America in 1995 by
Lynne Rienner Publishers, Inc.
1800 30th Street, Boulder, Colorado 80301

and in the United Kingdom by
Lynne Rienner Publishers, Inc.
3 Henrietta Street, Covent Garden, London WC2E 8LU

Library of Congress Cataloging-in-Publication Data
Toward civil society in the Middle East? : a primer / edited by
  Jillian Schwedler.
      p. cm.
    Includes bibliographical references.
    ISBN 1-55587-588-2 (pbk. : alk. paper)
    1. Middle East—Politics and government—1976– 2. Civil society—
Middle East. 3. Democracy—Middle East. 4. Political culture—
Middle East. 5. Islam and politics—Middle East. I. Schwedler,
Jillian.
JQ1758.A5T68 1995
306.2'0956—dc20   95-4613
                                                                      CIP

British Cataloguing in Publication Data
A Cataloguing in Publication record for this book
is available from the British Library.

Printed and bound in the United States of America

The paper used in this publication meets the requirements
of the American National Standard for Permanence of
Paper for Printed Library Materials Z39.48-1984.

5 4 3 2 1

Contents

Foreword

Augustus Richard Norton

Politics in the Middle East has long been refracted through geopolitical lenses that leave the observer with an image that is neither complete nor particularly accurate. Until recently, the overwhelming majority of books and articles on the region were not about the Middle East at all. Instead of being the subject, the region was typically the object of study, as authors—ever vigilant of stability—explored variants of an all-too-familiar theme: the struggle for the Middle East. Washington and Moscow, capitals of the Cold War camps jousting for influence and position, were obsessed with their zero-sum game, and serious examinations of the domestic determinants of politics in the region were superfluous. Moreover, when scholars focused on the Middle East, it was often to treat the Arab-Israeli conflict, the existential measure of a country's relevance for study; or the oil production of the Gulf, where the scholarly desideratum was weighed in 42-gallon barrels. With the Cold War now history and the Arab-Israeli conflict following suit, many analysts and scholars now turn their creative energies to the Islamist threat, a captivating example of reductionism if ever there was one.

This little book offers a clearer lens, one far less prone to distortion than the approaches cited. By introducing the study of civil society, this primer offers a different perspective on the Middle East, one that examines society in juxtaposition explicitly to the state, and implicitly to the fate of authoritarianism. In a region where freedom is often circumscribed and hollow, where governments are endemically suspicious of independent forms of association, civil society cannot be described as robust. This does not mean that civil society is absent. Associational life is richer in the Middle East than is commonly assumed, although there are significant variations among states, as well as among classes.

In the 1990s, civil society and, especially, the implied norms of civility and citizenship have become an important locus for debate inside and outside of the Middle East. This is a healthy debate that necessarily invokes crucial questions about the status of minorities, women, and the observance of human rights. Moreover, as Middle East governments face the arguably inescapable challenge of reform, it is becoming more widely recognized by policymakers as well as by scholars that if open forms of governments are to be made durable, they must be underpinned by a viable civil society. Absent a civil society, experiments in participatory forms of governments are unlikely to thrive. Of course, through their stultifying regulation and even suppression of associations, political parties, and clubs, the region's governments have often so distorted civil society that only ephemeral secular associations survive, thereby allowing the Islamist movements free reign.

Among the major observations emerging from many of the studies of the Civil Society Project in the Middle East Project is that the Islamist opposition has been strikingly successful in creating an array of organizations and associations that serve the needs of their constituents, especially among the urban poor. The challenge is to integrate Islamist associations into civil society. This challenge is crucial, since fostering a more viable, more inclusive, and more autonomous civil society will be a fool's errand for Middle East governments (and their external allies) unless the Islamist opposition is included. By the same token, unless the Islamists are willing to play by the rules of a civil society, it is hard to imagine their participation in the project of reform.

Civil society encompasses a wide swath of society and the Islamists are only part of the picture. In some settings, the Islamist opposition is a smaller part of the picture than many people may imagine; by exploring civil society one gains a sense of the rich array of associational forms found in a number of Middle Eastern settings. Cooperatives, unions, professional syndicates, women's movements, and a panoply of sporting clubs and informal circles are all relevant topics for examination. Not all of these components of civil society are in opposition to their governments, of course. Some of them benefit very handsomely from government support and see no need for change, others are apolitical, and yet others seek incremental political change.

The studies summarized here provide important insights into the workings of politics in the Middle East and give the reader a good sense of the breadth of the full-length studies found in the longer books produced by the Civil Society Project, which is also the sponsor of *Toward Civil Society in the Middle East?* In contrast to the status quo bias of earlier elite studies, the authors represented here are striving to look beyond the present, to develop a sense of what state-society relations may become as the Middle East enters the next millennium. Contrary to the ambiguities of political culture, the research into civil society has produced a wealth of solid empirical data.

This primer is a companion to *Quest for Change: Civil Society in the Middle East,* a documentary film that I produced in 1994 with Steve Talley.

I am confident that viewers of the film will be enriched by *Toward Civil Society in the Middle East?* By the same token, I am hopeful that viewers of the film will turn to this book for a guide to readings, as well as for a more thorough analysis of the themes that are introduced in the thirty-minute film.

The editor, Jillian Schwedler, has been a part of the Civil Society in the Middle East Project from its inception and for the past two years has been the program officer. She has assembled a remarkable collection of materials on civil society, ranging from seminal theoretical studies to unpublished reports. Her prowess in summarizing, analyzing, and describing contending perspectives on civil society is exemplified by the fine introduction that she has written for this volume. Countless students and many scholars will be in her debt for her distillation of a mountain of material, as well as for the yeowoman work she has performed in assembling the materials for this book.

Middle East governments are besieged by a plethora of problems, each one formidable in its own right. Cities are bursting at the seams, economies do not work very well, bureaucracies are neither responsive nor efficient, unemployment is rampant, and corruption is rife. Most important, people do not like their governments very much. Of course, rotten governments can totter on for a long time, and rulers may substitute repression for reform. Short-term political expediencies may be preferred to the fundamental changes that many scholars argue are necessary. As scholars, we may do no more than identify the strategic choices available to political leaders. The case for political reform is a strong one, and some Middle Eastern leaders will deduce (not necessarily accurately) that only through reform will they be able to preserve their power and privilege. When authoritarian governments navigate the shoals of change and open up space for civil society, this primer will be a good one to have in hand.

Preface

Three years ago, the Civil Society in the Middle East Project set out to answer many questions. By far the most important was, Is there such a thing as civil society in the Middle East? Not unexpectedly, public perception—shaped by Hollywood as much as by CNN and the rest of the media—was that a land as mysterious, barbaric, and hostile as the Middle East could not possibly be home to modern civil society. Perhaps most frustrating, however, was that a surprisingly large number of academics and regional specialists had the same response.

If this widespread misperception of the Middle East is ever to be overcome, it will begin with the realization that there is more to the region than religious zealotry and fanatical terrorism. As demonstrated by the individual case summaries in this book, there should be little doubt that there exists a wide range of associational activity in the Middle East that can be fairly called civil society. And as the many books and articles cited in the multilingual bibliography illustrate, the discussion of civil society is not limited to Western academic circles.

All interesting research questions in turn raise new questions, and the study of civil society has been no exception. How do the associations and social movements vary in character and strategy? To what extent do strong civil societies influence political reform? What is the nature of the relation, if any, between civil society and the transition to more representative governments? It is my hope that scholars, students, and policymakers will continue to explore these issues until we overcome the lingering image of the Middle East as backward, somehow less modern, than more developed regions.

Literally hundreds of people participated in the Civil Society in the Middle East Project. Nearly one hundred conference attendees, fifty anonymous manuscript referees, two dozen project authors, and ten graduate student interns joined project director Augustus Richard Norton, codirector Farhad Kazemi, and me to explore the existence, nature, and viability of civil society in the Middle East. Project participants hail from around the world and throughout the Middle East, and from a variety of disciplines and professions. In addition to those directly involved in the project, more than eight hundred scholars, students, diplomats, journalists, and policymakers subscribed to the project's monthly newsletter, the *Bulletin.* Hundreds of others attended project-sponsored panels, film premiers, and discussions at professional conferences and research institutes. Still others shared their thoughts by writing letters. This extensive participation provided ongoing feedback that helped shape the studies that appear in this and other project publications. Therefore, simply too many people played a role in what appears in this volume to thank individually.

New York University provided an institutional base for the project, and many people from the Kevorkian Center for Near Eastern Studies and the Department of Politics made that office a home. Without their support and the generous funding of the Ford and Rockefeller Foundations, the project would not have been possible. Many bright and talented people—from senior scholars and diplomats to young scholars and students—have become close colleagues and dear friends. I wish to thank each of them from the bottom of my heart for their difficult questions as much as their unfailing support.

Farhad Kazemi and Augustus Richard Norton have treated me, from the project's beginning, as a colleague and a friend. Together we have accomplished the work of a small army, cooperating in a way that will not be easily duplicated. They have perhaps done me a disservice by providing such a wonderful environment in which to work collaboratively and grow intellectually. I know I will look back at the good old days of the Civil Society Project, from the seventy-hour work weeks and blisters from rowing across Lake Como to the true spirit of cooperation and mutual respect that characterized our working atmosphere. I am deeply grateful to them both.

To Dick I owe special thanks: first, for recognizing my potential beyond that of a research assistant; and second, for holding me to the same high standards as he does himself. He has become a very dear friend, and I look forward to the time when I can even begin to thank him for all he has done for me.

Finally, I must thank my husband, Joel Sherman, my best and dearest friend in the whole world. Whether I am in Brooklyn or in Sana'a, you are my true inspiration.

J. M. S.

Introduction:
Civil Society and the
Study of Middle East Politics

Jillian Schwedler

Around the world, in Latin America, Eastern and Central Europe, Africa, and Asia, a surprising number of countries have made successful transitions to democratic forms of government. Many of these young democracies emerged with the collapse of the Soviet Union and the retreat of communism from Europe; others were created when regimes gave in to domestic pressure to hold national elections and, even more, to honor the results. There are many paths to democracy, few of which are smooth. However, it is a simple fact that the number of democratic, participant nations is steadily growing.

This trend toward democracy seems to have touched nearly every corner of the world. Argentina, Brazil, South Africa, Poland, and the Philippines are all examples of countries that have successfully made the transition to democracy. In other cases, such as Chile, Peru, Cambodia, Chad, Mozambique, and South Korea, political systems are gradually becoming more participant and pluralist, but strong opponents threaten to stall the process. More significant, however, is that this trend toward democracy has not been limited to one region or continent. Instead, pluralist, participant governments seem to be triumphing in nearly every part of the globe—with the exception of the Middle East. There, military despots struggle against Islamist reformers, but nowhere does the promise of pluralism appear to be part of the equation. Is the Middle East immune to the global trend toward democracy? Are Middle Easterners content to live under authoritarianism, whether secular or religious? Does the traditional, Islamic culture of the region simply prohibit the emergence of democracy?

To answer these questions, one must look beyond familiar images of the Middle East and approach the question of political reform from a new perspective. While one should not deny the intolerance of some groups, or the

1

authoritarian nature of many of the ruling regimes, these factors provide only part of the picture. Although they seldom receive attention in the West, hundreds of political parties, newspapers, radio stations, trade unions, and other organizations function outside of the government in virtually every Middle Eastern country. The existence of these nonstate actors raises important questions about whether they play a role in political reform.

A growing number of scholars have addressed this issue by exploring the relationship between civil society—this network of independent, voluntary organizations—and the prospects for nonviolent political reform, in general, and the emergence of democratic governments, in particular. Although the existence of civil society in the Middle East (or anywhere) does not mean that countries are on the verge of democratization, it does illustrate that citizens are both willing and able to play a role in shaping the state policies that govern their lives. And, as the experiences in Central and Eastern Europe illustrate, reform depends as much on the will of the citizens as on the willingness of the government.

The instances of civil society in the Middle East are not few. Every day, from Iran to Morocco and from Yemen to Turkey, citizens meet formally and informally to discuss issues ranging from health and social services to economic policy and political reform. Some Middle Eastern governments tolerate these gatherings; in other countries, nongovernmental associations are strictly forbidden and harshly repressed. Although the viability of such groups remains a contested issue, civil society in the Middle East has emerged as an important topic of debate among scholars, activists, policymakers, and citizens alike.

The idea that civil society exists throughout the Middle East is particularly valuable because it challenges lingering stereotypes of the region as traditional, primordial, and backward—that is, somehow less "modern" than Western countries and, hence, doomed to remain as such. These arguments continue to find an audience, but exploring civil society helps to dispel such myths: The large number of voluntary associations, overlooked or ignored in many analyses of the region, reveals a high level of political awareness, as well as deliberate, often sophisticated attempts to increase government accountability.[1]

But if civil society does exist within the Middle East, why are there so few, if any, truly representative and participant governments? Is the ineffectiveness of civil society due to a lack of effort on the part of citizens, or to governments' resolve to quash the voices of dissent? Studying civil society addresses broader power relations and political strategies in order to unpack a wide range of questions. For example, does the degree of political awareness and activism vary between men and women? Between urban and rural populations? The rich and the poor? The educated and the illiterate? How do state policies regulate and shape social organizations? And, perhaps most important, to what extent do state and social actors interact with tolerance and civility?

By exploring these and other questions, the collection of essays and case studies in this volume seeks to demonstrate that a broader understanding of state-society relations may provide important insights into the future of the region. In particular, civil society may reveal the prospects for society-generated political reform, that is, reform from below rather than above. This chapter will introduce the basic issues and arguments about the existence and emergence of civil society in the Middle East.

Conceptions of Civil Society

Political philosophers have been talking about civil society as long as they have been arguing over the state.[2] Even Plato had something to say about civil society. Since then, the term has been used in many different ways, too many to thoroughly review here.[3] For the purpose of this chapter, it is useful to explore two basic uses of the term "civil society": in classical political theory, and in contemporary debates.

Civil Society in Classical Political Theory

The term "civil society" began to appear regularly in political theory during the Enlightenment. In the work of the seventeenth-century English philosopher John Locke, for example, civil society played an important role as the sphere of social activity men[4] entered in order to protect their individual property rights.[5] This conception of civil society was developed by German philosophers who brought the term into common usage in their discussions of emerging capitalist countries. In their *burgerlichen gesellschaft* (civil society), *burgerlichen* captured the idea of both "civil" and "bourgeois." The organizations first identified as civil society—trade unions, professional associations, and employer associations—emerged primarily during the period of spreading industrialization and market capitalism in the eighteenth and nineteenth centuries. G. W. F. Hegel, a German philosopher of the early nineteenth century, argues that civil society developed as a means of protecting the individual rights and needs of the privileged to guarantee freedom in economic, social, and cultural spheres.[6] The organization and cooperation of various groups within civil society enable it to operate outside the state's coercive apparatus. As will become evident, civil society was not without its own internal coercion and intolerance.[7]

Civil society is also a sphere of mutual recognition and reciprocity; its purpose is to keep the state from interfering with the interests of its members, namely, the privileged bourgeoisie. It is not, however, a sphere identified exclusively with economic interests. Civil society is also, for Hegel, distinguished from political society, the sphere of political activity that includes political parties, public holdings, and government institutions.

Karl Marx, the nineteenth-century Prussian-born German philosopher, developed Hegel's idea of civil society to relate to changing forms of production within society:

> Civil society as such only develops with the bourgeoisie; the social organization evolving directly out of production and commerce.[8]

Hence, civil society not only facilitates, but develops alongside, capitalist expansion.

Antonio Gramsci, an Italian political theorist of the 1920s, further developed the idea of civil society as a system of control and exclusion. While the state (political society) is directly responsible for violent and coercive methods of control, civil society enables capitalists to exert control over social and economic practices through nonviolent means. That is, the state and civil society both exercise power over the whole of society, the former through physical force (or the threat of physical force), and the latter through control of the organizations of civil society.

Political society embodies the coercive nature of the state—through surveillance, a state police force, taxation, prisons, a legal system, and a state army—and civil society is the site of the ongoing struggle between the capitalists and laborers. It is the point of social praxis, the

> sphere of all the popular-democratic struggles which arise out of the different ways in which people are grouped together—by sex, race, generations, local community, region, nation and so on.[9]

In his early work on the public sphere, Jürgen Habermas argues that although civil society first emerges with the rise of capitalism, it soon develops a noneconomic, populistic component. As the organization of social labor shifts relations of economic domination away from the household, an independent sphere establishes itself "as the realm of commodity exchange and social labor governed by its own laws."[10] When civil society evolves, market activity comes to occupy a distinct upper tier—the bourgeois public sphere—and the lower tier of civil society is populated with organizations that challenge the state over noneconomic issues. As civil society gradually becomes more inclusive, however, the quality of public debate deteriorates to the point that interest-group politics—in which favor-swapping is commonplace—replace the original operational notion of the public sphere—in which the most persuasive argument prevails, regardless of its source. Habermas offers an explanation of why it is that in many contemporary societies, interest-group politics overwhelmingly characterize activity within the public sphere. Nevertheless, civil society must be understood fundamentally as a phenomenon of capitalist society that emerges as "activities and dependencies hitherto relegated to the framework of the household economy" shift outward to create a new sphere of activity between the private household and the state.[11]

Civil Society in Contemporary Debates

Much of the recent theoretical work on civil society has replaced the idea of civil society as a result of capitalist expansion with the idea that it is a sphere of democratic social interaction. The purpose of civil society is not to allow the bourgeoisie to protect their interests against encroachment from the state, but to enable all citizens to insure a degree of government accountability. The question of civil society becomes fundamental to the transition of authoritarianism to democracy.

For Guillermo O'Donnell and Philippe Schmitter, civil society emerges with the resurrection of the public sphere. In an effective authoritarian state, the regime in power seeks to "to orient most of their subjects toward the pursuit of exclusively private goals."[12] When individuals and groups begin to challenge the boundaries of permissible behavior—for example, by speaking out against the regime or demanding a government response to social needs—civil society begins to take shape.

The norms of equality, participation, tolerance, and political inclusion characterize activity within civil society. As a result, an active, vibrant civil society is an important quality-of-life gauge for every society. As Adam Ferguson argues, "The happiness of individuals is the great end of civil society: For, in what sense can a public enjoy any good, if its members, considered apart, be unhappy?"[13]

The boundaries of civil society have been broadened, as Habermas notes, to include virtually all nonviolent associational activity between individual citizens and the state. With this conceptualization of civil society as a median, the autonomous public sphere has proved enduring, and much attention has been focused on locating the boundaries of civil society. Edward Shils's view is typical:

> The idea of civil society is the idea of a part of society which has a life of its own, which is distinctly different from the state, and which is largely in autonomy from it. Civil society lies beyond the boundaries of the family and clan and beyond the locality; it lies short of the state.[14]

Here civil society refers to a sphere of pluralist activity, much of which seeks to directly challenge or limit the arbitrary use of state power. It is the protector of the individual against unjust government actions and policies as well as against encroachments from within civil society.

Civil society is not simply a sphere of activity outside of the state; it entails a set of rules governing behavior. As Sami Zubaida notes, it is the sphere of social mobilization in which "clear legislation and institutional mechanisms . . . provide the framework of rights and obligations."[15] For Larry Diamond, it is

> the realm of organized social life that is voluntary, self-generating, (large-ly) self-supporting, autonomous from the state, and *bound by a legal order or set of shared rules.*[16]

Consequently, the normative component of civil society is of central importance with regard to the behavior of individuals and organizations toward one another as well as between civil society groups and the government. As Jean Cohen and Andrew Arato argue in their comprehensive volume on civil society in political theory, civil society is more than the necessary and legitimate means of monitoring and controlling state authority and power: the "civil" behavior of members toward each other is central to distinguishing civil society from society in general. It is

> a sphere of social interaction between economy and state, composed above all of the intimate sphere (especially the family), the sphere of association (especially voluntary associations), social movements, and forms of public communication.[17]

Furthermore, civil society is not only pluralistic in its composition but democratic in its behavior. It does not refer solely to "rights to privacy, property, publicity (free speech and association), and equality before the law."[18] An additional ethical dimension is present, and this

> emphasis on the equal participation of everyone concerned in public discussions of contested political norms, obviously refers to the principles of democracy.[19]

In this way, the modern, liberal conception of civil society is fundamentally different from that of the classical theorists. Instead of the rights of individuals to amass property and pursue individual interests, civil society represents two ideals: first, the rights of each member of a community or nation to interact with a representative government; and, second, the establishment of a set of rules of acceptable, tolerant behavior between civil society and the state as well as within civil society. In particular, tolerance toward those with different views is paramount. Civil society embodies the question of "the proper mode of constituting society itself, whether in terms of private individuals or of a shared public sphere":[20] It is no less than the "virtuous" struggle for the "good life."[21] Adherence to these "rules of the game" will prove important to scholars seeking to identify the existence of civil society in specific regions or countries.

Debates on Civil Society in the Middle East

Scholarship on civil society in the Middle East has proliferated since the early 1980s. Analyses revolve around three key questions: First, does civil society even exist in the region?[22] Second, does it provide a challenge to existing government authority? And third, what sort of groups should be considered part of civil society?

Although the liberal democratic view of civil society has been adopted as a tool of inquiry for the Middle East, the term has been used to support two very distinct arguments: those who view civil society as weak or nonexistent, and those see civil society as the potential impetus for peaceful political reform.

Civil Society as Absent, Weak, or Disorganized

The first argument is that social groups challenging state power are either absent from the Middle East or largely ineffective. Until this deficiency is overcome, the argument goes, the region is virtually doomed to backwardness and persistent authoritarianism.[23] Many of these scholars are of the traditional school of Middle East studies, focusing on civilizational and cultural factors such as primordialism, traditionalism, and Islam as impediments to the emergence of more modern, participant, pluralist governments.[24]

Exemplifying this tradition, Elie Kedourie argues that challenges to state power are absent from the Middle East as a consequence of the region's Islamic tradition. In the West, he notes, "citizens organize themselves according to their various social, economic and political activities, in a multiplicity of groups and associations."[25] However,

> there is nothing in the political traditions of the Arab world—which are the political traditions of Islam—which might make familiar, or indeed intelligible, the organizing ideas of constitutional and representative government. The notion of the state . . . , the notion of popular sovereignty . . . , the idea of representation, of elections, of popular suffrage, of political institutions being regulated by laws laid down by a parliamentary assembly, . . . of society being composed of a multitude of self-activating, autonomous groups and associations—all of these are profoundly alien to the Muslim political tradition.[26]

Bernard Lewis draws a similar conclusion:

> Islamic history shows no councils or communes, no synods or parliaments, nor any other kind of elected or representative assembly. . . . There was no point, since the need for a procedure of corporate, collective decision never arose.[27]

Instead, the Middle East existed under an "ancient tradition of autocracy and acquiescence" until such ideas were introduced to the region in the aftermath of the French Revolution.[28]

Both Kedourie and Lewis argue that a limited number of independent social and political organizations exist in the Middle East, some of which indeed challenge state authority. These groups do not, however, make up a network that may be described as civil society, as they are not based on the shared idea of tolerance and pluralism.

Ernest Gellner offers a somewhat different view, combining culturalist and materialist analyses.[29] Still, he concludes that "the world of Islam" has not yet developed the necessary characteristic for the emergence of civil society—namely, secularization.

> The expectation of some additional Civil Society, which could hold the state to account, on top of the *Umma* defined as a shared commitment to the implementation of the Law, would seem almost impious, but in any case unrealistic. The state can be called to account for violation of the divinely ordained Law, or for the failure to implement it, but not for some additional requirements imposed by the popular as opposed to the divine will.[30]
>
> Islam . . . exemplifies a social order which seems to lack much capacity to provide political countervailing institutions or associations, which is atomized without much individualism, and operates effectively without intellectual pluralism.[31]

Newer generations of scholars draw similar conclusions without specifically identifying Arab or Islamic "culture" as the problem. Elia Zureik, for example, explicitly rejects the Orientalist focus on culture and religion as impediments to development, but he nonetheless concludes that Arab states had not, at least by the early 1980s, developed the institutions of civil society. State dominance, he argues, has been characteristic of the Arab state throughout its history, and "the absence of civil society (i.e., autonomous corporate institutions which operate with minimal state control) is an equally visible feature of Arab society."[32] Drawing on Gramsci, Zureik aims to understand the

> failure of the Arab State in terms of its inability to institutionalize corporate groups in society and ensure coordination in the relationship between civil and political society.[33]

Although the lack of civil society in the Middle East results from the failure of the Arab state to create such institutions, Arab societies also failed to organize in a way that would allow them to challenge state authority. Similarly, Peter Mansfield argues that the Middle East lacks a viable civil society because the organizations that do exist have been co-opted by the state to such an extent that they are virtually useless. There is, consequently, little prospect for change.[34]

This latter group of scholars distance themselves from the Orientalists who emphasize culture and civilization over political processes and struggles for power. They agree, however, that without strong challenges to despotic regimes, there is little hope for the emergence of more democratic politics in the region, at least in the foreseeable future.[35]

It is true that in much of the region, civil society has been the casualty of systematic efforts by the ruling authorities to decimate all potential opposition, a strategy particularly evident in the cases of Sudan and Iraq.[36] But the persistence of authoritarianism in the Middle East may have less to do with culture and tradition than with the political elite's desire to preserve its rule and the nature of other power relations in the society. This does not mean that social groups have failed to mount significant, nonviolent challenges to the ruling governments; it may only explain why so few have been successful.

Yet another group of scholars are skeptical of the usefulness of studying civil society in the Middle East. Unlike those already highlighted, these scholars do not question the existence of independent, voluntary associations in the region. Instead, they argue that the idea of civil society does not capture the diversity of these groups and their interactions with the state and with each other. Before addressing these questions, it will be useful to summarize the work of another group of scholars.

Civil Society as Emerging or Active

A small but growing number of scholars find the study of civil society in the Middle East useful precisely because it brings into question the idea that the region lacks the necessary social and political awareness to demand more inclusive political processes.[37] Looking beyond "cultural" explanations, this approach points to a wide variety of interest-based groups to illustrate that civil society not only exists in the Middle East, but is often quite vibrant.

As Michael Hudson notes, the

> hints of an expanding civil society constitute only circumstantial evidence; but . . . there are now enough such straws in the wind to indicate that important, politically relevant social changes are occurring.[38]

These social movements are not a new phenomenon. The activities, organization, and social bases of many such movements have been thoroughly explored.[39] Some scholars are even willing to argue that interest-based groups have been so effective that the "rules" of state-society interaction—although frequently manipulated by the political elite—have long been formalized. As Patricia Springborg notes,

> Not only does ancient Near Eastern society have the longest recorded history of civil and private law regarding the rights and property of the trader, but it likely pioneered the contractual forms in which they are expressed.[40]

Ellis Goldberg supports this view, pointing to the existence of civil society-like organizations in the Medieval Arab world.[41] But does focusing on the idea of civil society make these state-society relations more transparent?

It is worthwhile to note that the idea of civil society has gained wide currency in much of the Middle East, as much among policymakers and activists as scholars. As Eva Bellin notes,

> State officials in the Middle East use the term "civil society" to promote their projects of mobilization and "modernization"; Islamists use it to angle for a legal share of public space; and independent activists and intellectuals use it to expand the boundaries of individual liberty.[42]

One scholar who has embraced the civil society paradigm as a useful tool for the study of the contemporary Middle East is Augustus Richard Norton.[43] Noting that the region is replete with voluntary organizations, trade unions, human rights groups, women's associations, minority rights groups, and various other social organizations, he characterizes civil society as,

> the place where a mélange of groups, associations, clubs, guilds, syndicates, federations, unions, parties, and groups come together to provide a buffer between state and citizen.[44]

Exploring the strength and nature of communal associations should provide a more accurate picture of the Middle East than studies of authoritarianism or religious fundamentalism. Norton evokes the works of scholars whose use of the term "civil society" embodies the spirit of pluralism, democracy, and individual freedoms.[45] Similarly, Bellin notes that in all its diverse uses, the idea of civil society represents a challenge to despotism (which may, of course, be defined in very different ways).[46] Normative components are central: Civility, associability, and citizenship are identified by Norton as the three primary characteristics of civil society.[47] Civility is tolerance of the other, the idea that groups and individuals with very different ideas can live together in peace working within a representative and partic007-ipant system for their individual goals. Groups that do not play by the "rules of the game"—that is to say, those whose ultimate goal is to overthrow or replace the extant regime—are explicitly excluded from membership in civil society. Associability entails a spirit of cooperation, the idea that citizens can peacefully and openly organize around political issues, professions, or any common interest. Finally, citizenship is a crucial component that

> underpins civil society. To be a part of the whole is a precondition for the whole to be a sum of its parts. Otherwise, society has no coherence, it is just a vessel filled with shards and fragments. Thus, the individual in civil society is granted rights by the state, but, in return, acquires duties to the states.[48]

This approach is shared by scholars who have explored the existence and role of civil society in other regions. In her work on Africa, Naomi Chazan notes that groups that

> equate their own aims with those of the state and consequently seek to take it over (*some* fundamentalist groups, ethno-national movements, and ideological associations) are outside the bounds of civil society.[49]

But how might scholars classify which behavior is civil enough to fall into the realm of civil society? These normative criteria raise the question of what to do—at least theoretically—with groups that do not exhibit at least a modicum of civility, or adhere to the boundaries of "permissible" behavior. One might argue that extending the boundaries of civil society to include all peaceful means of contesting the existing political order diminishes the importance of civility and tolerance. Simply because an organization does not employ violent tactics does not necessarily mean that it respects the rights of other competing organizations to promote different objectives. The issue, as Norton notes, is behavioral and not psychological. What matters is not how people feel about others, but how they act toward them.

It may be useful here to look to political thinkers who define political society as distinct from civil society, as do Hegel and Gramsci. For them, civil society, as the sphere where citizens seek to protect specific interests, is distinct from political society, where both government institutions and groups such as political parties seek to play a direct role in government. This is only a theoretical distinction, of course, as some groups may play both roles. During the Gulf War, for example, Kuwaiti professional associations, religious groups, and cooperative societies mobilized as resistance to the Iraqi occupation.[50] However, exploring the distinction between political society and civil society may help clarify questions concerning how to define acceptable behavior as well as the extent to which the government honors its own rules and commitments to its citizens.

The basic question is whether those organizations that may seek to one day replace the state should be counted as actors within civil society on the basis that their current behavior is peaceful, tolerant, and within the "rules of the game." The question should not be whether they seek to reform or change the government, but whether they seek to do so by working within the system. This is a very sensitive issue, particularly with regard to Islamist organizations. These groups may be playing fairly now, critics argue, but will they dismantle democratic institutions once they have gained sufficient power?

This problem, the age-old paradox of democracy, is not unique to the Middle East.[51] Democratic political processes may legitimately yield a government that seeks to replace democratic institutions with a less pluralist, inclusive, or representative system. In the Middle East, the 1992 elections in Algeria, which were aborted precisely because of this fear, have stirred much debate in this regard.[52] Farhad Kazemi and Norton argue, however, that government strategies of inclusion are likely to have a moderating effect on political movements, and strategies of exclusion leave opposition groups with little choice but to adopt radical or revolutionary stances.[53] Therefore, all groups that behave within the "rules of the game" must be considered legitimate actors within civil society.

The concept of civil society is employed in a somewhat narrower sense by Saad Eddin Ibrahim, for whom civil society in the Middle East comprises the secular, nongovernmental organizations that are emerging as important political actors throughout the region.[54] As such, Islamist groups are categorically excluded, although they often use the channels of civil society to further their own agendas.

Ibrahim emphasizes the importance of placing the emergence of civil society in the Middle East in historical context. The nation-state and civil society have historically evolved simultaneously, and neither is fully autonomous from the other. Furthermore, European colonialism played a critical role in the current political ordering of the Middle East, specifically the emergence of a "new social contract" and the crisis of legitimacy that many regimes now face.[55] The importance of historicism for the study of civil society in the Middle East will be further discussed later in this chapter.

Despite these concerns, Ibrahim is in accord with Bellin, Kazemi, and Norton, arguing that employing the idea of civil society in the study of the Middle East may shed light on a wide variety of voluntary, interest-based organizations that are often overlooked in analyses of political reform in the region.[56] But the question of whether Islamist organizations should be considered an integral part of civil society remains a sensitive and central question for debates on civil society throughout the region.

Civil Society and Islamist Organizations

In recent years, Islamist[57] groups have been among the most effective political actors to challenge state authority in the Middle East, more often through the provision of basic social services than through armed struggle against the state or political terrorism.[58] At the same time, the objectives and activities of Islamist organizations vary markedly, and some advocate the overthrow of governments to establish Islamic regimes that would govern according to the *shari'ah,* or Islamic law. As a result, many scholars have concluded that Islam and democracy are fundamentally irreconcilable. Kedourie argues, for example, that there is

> a deep confusion in the Arab public mind, at least about the meaning of democracy. The confusion is, however, understandable since the idea of democracy is quite alien to the mind-set of Islam.[59]

But the question should not be about whether an Islamic state is democratic, but about the differences in behavior and tactics among self-proclaimed Islamist organizations.[60] As John Esposito argues, the image of the looming threat of Islamic fundamentalism draws on stereotypes, half-truths, and attempts to identify a new global threat to democracy in the wake of the Cold War.[61] "Islamist movements"—a term used to describe groups as disparate as political parties, healthcare providers, terrorist groups, and social clubs—vary significantly in their objectives and strategies, and as such do not constitute a monolith. If this is true, can such differences be addressed through the civil society paradigm?

Norton directly addresses this question by making a categorical distinction between moderate and radical Islamists.[62] On the one hand, "moderate" Islamists are those who reject violent, revolutionary tactics and choose to work for reform through existing political channels and processes, such as parliamentary elections and judicial review. "Radical" Islamists, on the other hand, seek to take control of the state by force.

Kazemi and Norton take this argument further, arguing that participation in democratic political processes and peaceful coexistence with those holding different views are sufficient conditions to consider any organization, Islamist or otherwise, a valuable part of civil society.[63] This approach does not suggest that all Islamist groups fit nicely into the civil society paradigm; rather, it seeks to capture the spirit of participation in legitimate political processes, of which Islamist organizations are one integral part. As Talal Asad argues, even in

a secular, liberal state that subscribes to the principles of religious toleration, historical religions (including secularized versions of religious traditions) are part of civil society.[64]

Of course, political inclusion is not without its tensions; but, secular and
religious coexistence is a feature of even liberal secular states.

Carrie Rosefsky-Wickham challenges Kazemi and Norton's categorical distinction between moderate and radical Islamists. In Egypt, she
argues,

> mainstream Islamist groups play by the rules of the present social and
> political order, yet their ultimate goal is to transform it from the bottom up.
> That is, they aim not to establish a civil sphere separate from and coexis-
> tent with the secular state, but gradually to extend the Islamic domain until
> it encompasses the state itself.[65]

Like Ibrahim, Rosefsky-Wickham notes that these thoroughly modern
Islamist movements have been savvy in using legitimate political processes
to challenge the dominant political order. Local and national elections, for
example, have offered Islamists entry into official state political processes.[66]
But she seems to disagree with Kazemi and Norton about whether the participation of these Islamist groups threaten democracy. At the very least,
their participation challenges those individuals who have a vested interest in
maintaining the status quo—and those interested in maintaining the status
quo often prefer that political processes remain undemocratic. Still, Kazemi
and Norton conclude, the participation of the most viable opposition groups
may offer the greatest incentives for states to liberalize their political
processes: Inclusion enables the state to regulate and monitor all groups that
are full players in civil society and tends to moderate the rhetoric and objectives of the groups that opt for participation. It is precisely a victory for representative institutions that many Islamist groups are promoting social and
political transformation through democratic channels, rather than revolution. Consequently, Kazemi and Norton argue, participation should be
encouraged rather than shunned with suspicion.

What does all this say about whether Islamist groups should be counted
as actors within civil society? To exclude Islamist organizations would be to
ignore the fact that they have been among the most effective means of challenging government authority and responding to citizens' needs and concerns. Yet, to include Islamist groups as part of civil society may overlook
fundamental differences in political aspirations that even a categorical distinction between moderates and radicals does not fully capture. To be sure,
some Islamist organizations operate with the utmost civility and tolerance,
while others do not allow differences of opinion even among their own
members. Any analysis of social movements in the Middle East—whether or

not conducted under the civil society paradigm—must pay careful attention to the nature of each individual organization and avoid characterizing all groups on the basis of the activities of a few.

Critiques of the Study of Civil Society in the Middle East

Many scholars have been critical of attempts to study civil society in the Middle East. Having just surveyed the arguments of those who have applied the concept of civil society to the Middle East, we can now address several associated theoretical and methodological issues.

Is the Idea of Civil Society Too Historically Specific?

Is it appropriate to employ theoretical concepts that originated in Western political thought to non-Western societies? Some scholars argue that because historical experiences vary markedly, exporting concepts from the historical context in which they emerged may obscure more than is revealed. This is a valid concern, particularly when the resulting analysis looks something like this:

1. Civil society comprises voluntary organizations such as trade unions, professional associations, and minority rights groups.
2. Since such groups in the Middle East are few in number and generally ineffective, civil society is, for all practical purposes, nonexistent in the region.

This sort of reasoning—judging societies in terms of the degree to which certain "modern" institutions have developed—is not uncommon in Middle Eastern studies. By assuming that all societies can and should emulate the model of the industrialized West, one can easily label regions that do not resemble their Western counterparts as "traditional," "underdeveloped," and "backward." But since it is unreasonable to expect all societies to share a common social trajectory—that is, to evolve in a similar manner—the limits and biases of this sort of approach should be obvious.

The failings of poor analyses, however, should not be construed as a fundamental weakness of comparative political theory. Instead of abandoning the idea of civil society, some scholars have asked, "What is it that civil society achieves vis-à-vis the state?" As Hudson notes,

> Civil society interpreted in specifically Western (Lockean, Hegelian, Weberian or Marxist) terms is unlikely to emerge in the Middle East, but this should not exclude the development of other kinds of inclusive solidarity communities.[67]

Focusing on the function of civil society, rather than specific structures, one can ask, "What sort of groups in the Middle East—be they familial, professional, tribal, religious, clan-based, or whatever—fulfill the function of civil society?" How do citizens and communities address their interests or grievances vis-à-vis government policies? When the question is framed this way, the idea of civil society may highlight a wide range of social interactions that might otherwise be dismissed as irrelevant. In this sense, civil society indeed exists throughout the Middle East. Where civil society is weak, it is often the result of government oppression rather than deficiencies within the societies themselves. Thus, although the import of Western concepts into non-Western contexts raises important methodological concerns, cautious and careful application may nonetheless advance research on the contemporary Middle East. The importance of these historical differences should not be underestimated.

Still, employing the concept of civil society can be particularly problematic when the history of social and political forces of the region in question is strikingly different than those under which the concept emerged. As Dwayne Woods emphasizes in his study of Africa, civil society reflects a specific vision of state-society relations:

> The development of civil society in Europe was the result of an empirical differentiation between public and private interests as well as the idealization of this separation.[68]

The idea of civil society is the idea of a particular means of using public space, institutionalized by the constitutional state.[69] The rise of the nation-state as the dominant political unit accompanied the growth of global market capitalism, supported by modern, rational law. The result was a gradual reordering of society, which allowed for the emergence of new spheres of action, rather than simply extending state control over existing communal associations.[70] Consequently, use of the concept of civil society may offer fewer insights in regions where a similar differentiation between public and private is not idealized.

Likewise, Adam Seligman argues that the idea of civil society cannot be understood outside of its original context, namely, the Enlightenment. The coherence of the idea of civil society was specific to that time, and use of the term as a model for contemporary social organization—in both Western and non-Western contexts—is highly problematic because it neglects these roots:

> It was precisely . . . reason and revelation—and a unique, fragile and historically contingent balance between them that infused the original notion of civil society with its overwhelming saliency, but which today can no longer provide the ground for contemporary arguments for civil society.[71]

The idea of a public sphere hinges on the existence of a parallel private space: "Both must exist in dialectic unity for sense to be made of either one."[72] But because the nature of exchange within civil society is "rooted in a sphere of values predicated on the mutuality of individual recognition," civil society can only be understood as a particularistic moral vision.[73] As a result, any export of the term as a conceptual tool will necessarily be problematic.

This concern is addressed within the context of Middle East studies by Şerif Mardin, who calls civil society a "Western dream" and a "historical aspiration." Civil society is

> the idea that social relations are both sustained and energized by autonomous, secular collectives with legal personality operative within a frame of rationalized law.[74]

This particular structural manifestation of human agency was conceived in Western social history, driven by the dream of transforming a utopian ideal into reality. Civil society did not, Mardin argues, have a structural equivalent in the Islamic cultures of the Middle East until colonialist projects disrupted the region's social-political trajectory.

Mardin suggests that instead of looking for civil society in the Middle East, one should seek to identify the "dream" of both Western and Islamic societies and ask whether they are comparable.[75] The Muslim social dream is based on a vision of society mandated by God through a charismatic intermediary; its humanistic content is based on an Islamic vision, one that precludes the idea of man as perfectible or in control of his own destiny.[76] Although this Islamic dream is no less civil than the Western image of civil society, it was not driven by rational-legalism, but by a force that was charismatic during the prophet Muhammad's lifetime and divine following his death.[77] Consequently, one must explore both Islamic ideology and the historical forces that guided political behavior and determined the appropriate use of public space to understand the social organizations that occupy the public sphere in the Middle East today.[78]

The emergence of the "idea" of civil society, as Mardin argues, must be seen in the context of a gradual incorporation of the Middle East into the capitalist world economy dominated by Western nations. The organizations that existed earlier filled the function of civil society but were not viewed as a sphere of social activity in the way civil society is under the modern nation-state system.

The challenge to existing means of utilizing public space was—indeed, is—for interest groups to learn to use state-approved avenues for the contestation of power and state policies without becoming appropriated or manipulated by the state. Throughout the region, new government regulations limiting the form and nature of political parties, interest-based organizations, or charitable associations, have constricted the ability of precolonialist associations (religious, communal, tribal, familial, etc.) to function effectively. (Interestingly, many of these precolonialist groups are now among the most effective.) As a result, some of the associational life in the Middle East has slowly begun to resemble its counterparts in other regions, including the West.

Simon Bromley challenges this view of intersecting social and political trajectories. The Middle East was not, he argues, a region "existing outside of, and developing independently from, Europe, only entering the Western orbit with the finding of oil and the formation of the state of Israel."[79] However,

> all too often, the active, determining role of the European powers in the political, economic and cultural formation of the region is neglected in favor of a simplistic emphasis on resources and religion.[80]

Others also argue that Western colonialism did not introduce the sort of social mobilization characterized as civil society; instead, it led to the dissolution of the existing Arab civil societies. As Hanna Batatu argues, European colonizers in Iraq destroyed the participatory social institutions of civil society, leaving the earlier social order in shambles and creating new, colonialist institutions in their place.[81]

Others have agreed that the Middle East has a long history of civil society, in its functional sense, pointing to evidence of the existence and effectiveness of interest-based organizations (often trade associations), their role vis-à-vis the ruling authority, and the institutionalization of rules and regulations governing these interactions. Springborg, for example, illustrates that the Middle East has "a long history of civil and private law."[82] Goldberg stresses that even during Medieval times, the Arab world was characterized by a rich associational life closely resembling civil society. Contemporary analyses, he argues, can posit the absence of civil society only by overlooking compelling evidence of its existence:

> Only if we assume medieval Muslims were incredibly stupid or if we are willing ourselves to be exceptionally obtuse can we assert that there was no civil society in a world in which men . . . managed to assert claims to and defend their property from kings on a systematic basis.[83]

The State-Civil Society Boundary: Define or Deconstruct?

In various studies of civil society throughout the world, many scholars have sought to identify precisely where civil society ends and where the state begins. There are two basic approaches to this question. The predominant approach addresses the nature of the relationship between the state and civil society, defining the criteria by which any particular organization or institution should be considered part of the state or part of civil society. An alternative approach seeks to question the very notion that such a distinction exists and explore the power structures that are hidden behind the idea of autonomy between civil society and the state as well as alternate social structures operating within the region.

Most scholars provide some theoretical criteria to distinguish between the state and civil society. Shils, for example, notes that "autonomy vis-à-vis the state is one of the features of civil society."[84] Although the two must be understood as distinct entities,

> civil society and the state are bound together by the constitution and by traditions which stress the obligations of each to the other as well as their rights vis-à-vis each other.[85]

Keane argues that this state-civil society boundary has become even more pronounced in recent years.[86]

This approach raises several questions that need to be explored both theoretically and empirically: What is the nature of the relationship between state and civil society actors? What are the norms that guide behavior between the two? Do these norms vary between countries and localities? What happens when actors from one or both of these spheres depart from these norms? To what extent do state actors honor these norms under uncertain or challenging conditions (e.g., when an unsavory opponent seems to be winning elections)?

Central to the concept of civil society, Shils argues, is the idea of mutual adherence to the norm of civility that "regulates the conduct between individuals and between individuals and the state."[87] The existence of civil society thus depends upon broader state-society relations and norms.

In this approach, the link between the emergence of civil society and the potential for democratic transformation is often made explicit. Gellner notes that civil society and democracy are often used somewhat synonymously, but that "civil society" is a preferable term to describe events such as the transformation of Eastern Europe since 1985 and the abortive coup in Moscow in August 1991.[88]

> Because it highlights those institutional pre-conditions and the necessary historical context, "Civil Society" is probably a better, more illuminating slogan than "democracy."[89]

Likewise, O'Donnell and Schmitter argue that transition from authoritarian rule entails not only the triumph of "soft-liners" over "hard-liners," but also the "resurrection of civil society." Authoritarian regimes are often successful when they manage to turn the attention of individual citizens away from matters of public concern and "withdraw into private pursuits and set aside, prudently ignore, or even forget their public and political identities."[90] Civil society begins to reemerge when the government signals a willingness to allow room for some limited political contestation. However—and this is critical for O'Donnell and Schmitter's analysis—

> the catalyst in this transformation often comes first from exemplary individuals, who begin testing the boundaries of behavior initially imposed by the incumbent regime. . . . In the precarious public spaces of the first stages of the transition, these individual gestures are astonishingly successful in provoking or reviving collective identification and actions; they, in turn, help forge broad identifications which embody the explosion of a highly repoliticized and angry society.[91]

Thus, the impetus for political reform comes from outside of the government, by individuals or groups that provide the seed for the emergence or resurrection of civil society. It is soft-liners or moderates within the regimes that see the benefits of gradually loosening constraints on associability and political contestation, but such a strategy is attractive only in the face of increased pressure from within society.

The logic of this argument—that political liberalism, if not democracy itself, can be furthered through the development of civil society—has begun to take root in the field of Middle East studies. For Norton, the causal relationship is transparent: "The functioning of civil society is literally and plainly at the heart of participant political systems"; it is "a necessary, though not sufficient condition for the development of democracy."[92] Civil society alone is insufficient because a responsible state apparatus is required to ensure that the groups that compose civil society behave with civility, toward each other as well as toward the state. "Unless government plays a controlling or intermediary role, the result is likely to be chaos."[93] In fact, according to Norton, it is "meaningless to speak of civil society in the absence of the state."[94]

Thus, in this view the realization of a more liberal, participant Middle East requires at least limited cooperation between the state and civil society. Disparate voices from civil society should help shape state policy while the state serves as administrator and regulator to ensure fair play. The existence of legal-institutional guarantees for freedom of speech, movement, and assembly may even be necessary for the emergence of civil society.[95] In this regard, many governments in the region have indeed begun to slowly liberalize, and the organs of civil society in the region seem to have become increasingly active. However, correlation does not equal causation, and the existence of a strong, active civil society may not ensure equality of access to political channels and the protection of civil rights for all segments of a population, particularly across class, gender, and racial divides. As Hudson notes,

> An opening by the state and regime that is confined only to a small upper middle class constituency may actually prove to be retrogressive by criteria of equity and redistribution.[96]

In fact, it is often the case that the ruling elite seek to protect their interests by directly defining what constitutes civil society and by establishing and maintaining the rules governing behavior within the public sphere. As Alberto Melucci notes, the

> needs and forms of action arising from the society are not easily adaptable to the existing channels of political participation and to the organizational forms of political agencies.[97]

The political elite clearly have a vested interest in maintaining channels they can regulate. By promoting the idea that civil society—indeed, all of society—possesses a considerable degree of autonomy from official state institutions, they may present the image of a truly participant and representative society without sacrificing any real power.[98] In Jordan, for example, King Hussein champions the participation of political parties in the country's multiparty elections. Behind the scenes, however, he manipulated the electoral process to undercut the strength of the Islamic Action Front, a group that made considerable gains through official political channels.[99]

So, the state may allow a certain amount of space to some organizations, or quash existing groups and construct parallel, state-controlled organizations in their place, as in Syria and Egypt.[100] In some cases, as in Iraq and the Sudan, governments have actively dismantled the organs of civil society and restricted the emergence of new organizations. As Rosefsky-Wickham notes, the impact of the shift from one-party rule to pluralism

> is limited so long as the political party's contestation is tightly controlled from above and emergency laws remain in effect.[101]

As the maker of rules and the keeper of order in the society, the ruling elite may have moved beyond Weber's vision of the state as possessing a monopoly on the legitimate use of violence, to a more subtle and coercive role under the guise of guarantor of constitutional law in a society ruled by social contract.

If this is the case, the view of a clear distinction between the civil society and the state—to the extent that the former is seen to provide a "buffer" between the citizen and the state—is somewhat problematic. As Seligman notes, "the public/private divide is a . . . serious problem, which brings us to the heart of the image of civil society as a moral vision."[102] That is, the idea of a boundary between the state and civil society is purely theoretical, and should not be presumed to actually exist in any society. As Timothy Mitchell argues,

> the elusiveness of the state-society boundary needs to be taken seriously, not as a problem of conceptual precision but as a clue to the nature of the phenomenon.[103]

The idea of the state as distinct from society

> must be taken not as the boundary between two discrete entities, but as a line drawn internally within the network of institutional mechanisms through which a social and political order is maintained.[104]

Locating this imaginary boundary is problematic in the Middle East precisely because there is no such clear distinction in the West or anywhere.

This raises a problem for O'Donnell and Schmitter's analysis concerning their argument that the resurrection of civil society is sparked by individuals outside of the public sphere who decide to test the boundaries of permissible behavior. Do these "exemplary individuals" simply awaken one day with an inclination to stir things up? Or, do they emerge through existing and shifting systems of power? They emerge, according to O'Donnell and Schmitter, from the intelligentsia, professional associations, religious groups, and other existing organizations (which do not collectively compose "civil society" until they collectively challenge state authority).[105] The idea of a give-and-take between the state and certain individuals or groups marks the decline of authoritarianism and the resurrection of civil society.

But their idea of "layers of an explosive society" suggests the existence of alternative systems of power, which O'Donnell and Schmitter explore only to the extent that they yield remarkable individuals who dare reenter the public sphere. The existence of these alternate systems, however, seems to contradict the claim that under authoritarianism, citizens withdraw from, or are forced out of, the public sphere. Instead, what seems to happen is that citizens withdraw from one particular system of power, namely, the public sphere regulated by the state.

Rather than view the public sphere as the only avenue to social mobilization, it is more useful to view it as only one of many such channels or systems of power. Likewise, the individuals or groups that enter civil society do not simply materialize from thin air; instead, they emerge from these alternative systems of power. As Melucci argues, social movements (or "remarkable" individuals) should not be treated as simply empirical phenomena to record. Social movements are action systems:

action *systems* in that they have structures . . . *action* systems in that their structures are built by aims, beliefs, decisions, and exchanges operating in a systemic field.[106]

For the study of the Middle East, this sort of approach may prove more useful for understanding and analyzing diverse Islamist movements, for example, by locating them within alternative power systems, rather than simply judging each to be either inside or outside of civil society.[107] Thus, the interaction between the state and civil society—of governments maneuvering to deflate potential threats to their stability, on the one hand, and on the other hand, organizations responding, positively or negatively, to these new and changing "rules of the game"—is only one of many such dynamic processes of power relations, namely, that of the modern nation-state. As Asad notes,

> the attempt to establish fixed boundaries between populations, to reform and standardize their beliefs and practices, to secure their loyalties, and to define their community membership—all this has been central to the project of the modern nation-state. . . . It is the distinctive character of the modern state's strategic and administrative disciplines.[108]

A further problem of taking the state/society dichotomy as natural, rather than constructed, is that one may conclude erroneously that state-society interaction is less a dynamic process than a zero-sum game.[109]

So, if a boundary between the state and civil society does not exist, how useful is the idea of civil society as an analytical tool? It is first important to remember that "civil society" does not *really* exist anywhere; it is only an abstract idea, a theoretical construct. As such, it should be viewed and used as a tool to facilitate analysis, not as an actual phenomenon to record and analyze. Norton cautions that it is this confusion of the real world with the ideal type that has led some scholars to draw disappointing conclusions about the prospects for civil society.[110] In Middle East studies, the idea of civil society is useful only to the extent that it facilitates the understanding of actual social and political phenomena, power structures, and state-society relations.[111] No single approach can explain every phenomenon, and the study of civil society is no exception. Whether the results are progressive in the sense that they explain more than existing scholarship is a judgment that each person must make individually.

Conclusion

To return to the questions posed at the beginning of this chapter, is the Middle East immune to the global trend toward democracy? Are Middle

Easterners content to live under authoritarianism, whether secular or religious? Does the traditional, Islamic culture of the region simply prohibit the emergence of democracy? Studies of civil society in the region argue that, for each question, the answer is clearly no.

First, the Middle East is not immune to the global trend toward democracy. There have been numerous instances of controlled political reform in which citizens have been gradually brought into the political processes not only through civil society, but through direct, legitimate elections.

Second, Middle Easterners are not content to live under authoritarianism. The wide range of civil society organizations and the emergence of alternative political parties illustrate that Middle Eastern citizens are not only politically aware but motivated in their desire to play a direct role in their government. Although different groups call for different types of reform, in each case the demand is for change.

Third, the so-called obstacles to political reform that exist in a traditional culture, such as that of the Middle East, are neither ancient nor obstacles. The region itself is quite diverse, and no one country or area should be expected to progress or modernize in the same way as any other. In particular, Islam should not be seen as an obstacle to democracy. Certain groups may oppose certain paths of political reform, but it is individual movements, and not Islam itself, that are the obstacles. Indeed, there are a number of Islamist groups in the region that have accepted democratic processes as a legitimate means of political reform.

Many governments in the Middle East—particularly those unable to provide basic social services to their people—are allowing for gradual political inclusion as a direct response to demands from civil society. Sometimes, these strategies of inclusion should be viewed critically as efforts by the ruling elite to weaken oppositional movements by incorporating them into state-regulated processes—all the while presenting a moderate, democratic face to concerned foreign-aid grantors. Although scholars continue to disagree about the effectiveness of civil society in bringing about political reform, both the hopeful and the skeptical agree that the emergence of civil society facilitates peaceful public expression of political preferences and grievances, while also providing weak or threatened governments with "breathing room" in which to regroup.

Only time will show whether the growth of civil society ultimately leads to more participant, representative politics, or further entrenches the political and economic elite. However, as the study of civil society in the Middle East illustrates, citizens throughout the region are actively pursuing more inclusive and participant political processes. Like people throughout the world, they wish to have a say in how they are governed.

Notes

Limited portions of this chapter were adapted from "Conceptions of Civil Society: Islam and Political Participation in the Middle East," presented at the Middle East Studies Association 1993 annual meeting at Research Triangle Park, North Carolina. In addition to the participants in that panel session, I wish to express my thanks to Laurie Brand, Farhad Kazemi, Timothy Mitchell, Augustus Richard Norton, and John Vantine for their thoughtful comments on earlier drafts. All errors and failings are my own.

1. Most of the individual country summaries in this volume appear full-length in Norton, *Civil Society in the Middle East,* vols. 1 & 2.

2. The idea of civil society is meaningless outside of broader theories of the state. See Cohen and Arato, *Civil Society and Political Theory,* who deal comprehensively with the question of state-society relations in their 771-page book; and Keane, *Civil Society and the State,* especially his chapter on "Despotism and Democracy: The Origins and Development of the Distinction Between Civil Society and the State." For theories of the state, see Carnoy, *The State and Political Theory;* Migdal, Kohli, and Shue, *State Power and Social Forces: Domination and Transformation in the Third World;* Evans, Rueschemeyer, and Skoçpol, *Bringing the State Back In;* Almond, "The Return to the State"; Nettl, "The State as a Conceptual Variable"; and Mitchell, "The Limits of the State: Beyond Statist Approaches and Their Critics."

3. In addition to Cohen and Arato, *Civil Society and Political Theory,* and Keane, *Civil Society and the State,* see Seligman, *The Idea of Civil Society;* Gellner, *Conditions of Liberty: Civil Society and Its Rivals;* Keane, *Democracy and Civil Society;* Shils, "The Virtue of Civil Society"; Walzer, "The Idea of Civil Society"; and Diamond, "Rethinking Civil Society: Toward Democratic Consolidation."

4. For an excellent discussion of the gender discrimination of various conceptualizations of civil society, see Pateman, "The Fraternal Social Contract." Pateman explores the "silence about the part of the story which reveals that the social contract is a fraternal pact that constitutes civil society as a patriarchal or masculine order" (p. 101). Also see "Gender and Civil Society," an interview with Suad Joseph.

5. See Locke, *Two Treatises on Government;* and Seligman, *The Idea of Civil Society,* who discusses Locke's conceptualization of civil society in detail.

6. See Hegel, *Philosophy of Right.*

7. Asad, "Religion and Politics: An Introduction," p. 7, footnote 7.

8. Marx, *The Marx-Engels Reader,* p. 163.

9. See Simon, *Gramsci's Political Thought: An Introduction.*

10. See Habermas, *The Structural Transformation of the Public Sphere: An Inquiry into a Category of Bourgeois Society;* and the series of response essays in Calhoun, *Habermas and the Public Sphere.*

11. Habermas, *The Structural Transformation,* p. 19.

12. O'Donnell and Schmitter, *Tentative Conclusions About Uncertain Democracies,* p. 48.

13. See Ferguson, *An Essay on the History of Civil Society.*

14. Shils, "The Virtue of Civil Society," p. 3.

15. Zubaida, "Islam, the State, and Democracy: Contrasting Conceptions of Society in Egypt."

16. Diamond, "Rethinking Civil Society: Toward Democratic Consolidation," p. 5 (emphasis added).

17. Cohen and Arato, *Civil Society and Political Theory,* p. ix. Cohen and Arato's own definition of civil society includes family and familial networks, but excludes the organs of the market, which should be distinguished from civil society as economic society (p. x). This separation of society into political, civil, and economic spheres (Hegel combined the latter two) is original to Cohen and Arato. For a contrasting view, in which political and economic society are portions of a broader civil society, see Walzer, "The Idea of Civil Society."

18. Ibid., p. 345.

19. Ibid., p. 345.

20. Seligman, *The Idea of Civil Society,* p. 2.

21. Shils, "The Virtue of Civil Society," p. 1; and Walzer, "The Idea of Civil Society," pp. 293–304, respectively.

22. The term "civil society" is most frequently translated into Arabic as *al-mujtama' al-madani,* commonly so in Egypt. At the conference on "Civil Society and the Prospects for Political Reform in the Middle East" (sponsored by the Civil Society in the Middle East project and convened at the Aspen Institute Wye Conference Center in Queenstown, MD, 30 September–2 October 1994), Nazih Ayubi noted that *al-mujtama' al-madani* was perhaps less preferable a translation than *al-mujtama' al-ahali.* Since *al-madani* is closer in meaning to "civic," it may be understood to refer only to secular organizations. *Al-ahali* may be preferable as it more closely captures the term "civil," and as such would include Islamist and other religious groups that adhere to accepted standards of civility and tolerance.

23. For an overview and critical analysis of the philosophical roots of Orientalist views of civil society in the Middle East, see Springborg, *Western Republicanism and the Oriental Prince.* For an excellent discussion of authoritarianism in the region, see Crystal, "Authoritarianism and Its Adversaries in the Arab World."

24. This traditional school of Middle East studies is frequently referred to as "Orientalism"—in the pejorative sense of Said's seminal *Orientalism.*

25. Kedourie, *Democracy and Arab Political Culture,* p. 4.

26. Ibid., pp. 5–6. Also see Wittfogel, *Oriental Despotism.*

27. Lewis, *The Shaping of the Modern Middle East,* pp. 45–46.

28. Ibid., p. 46.

29. This characterization of Gellner's approach belongs to Bromley, *Rethinking Middle East Politics,* pp. 24–30.

30. Gellner, *Conditions of Liberty: Civil Society and Its Rivals,* p. 28.

31. Ibid., p. 29.

32. Zureik, "Theoretical Considerations for a Sociological Study of the Arab State," p. 256.

33. Ibid., p. 255.

34. See Mansfield, *A History of the Middle East.*

35. See Sadowski, "The New Orientalism and the Democracy Debate."

36. Lesch, "The Destruction of Civil Society in the Sudan" (summary included in this volume); and al-Khalil, *The Republic of Fear.*

37. Several scholars have pointed to the emergence of more participant political systems in the Middle East as potential signs that governments in the region are edging toward more democratic politics. See, for example, Hudson, "Democratization and the Problem of Legitimacy in Middle East Politics."

38. Ibid., p. 164.

39. See, for example, Beinin and Lockman, *Workers on the Nile: Nationalism, Communism, Islam, and the Egyptian Working Class;* Bianchi, *Unruly Corporatism: Associational Life in Twentieth-Century Egypt;* Cole, *Colonialism and Revolution in*

the Middle East; Denoeux, *Urban Unrest in the Middle East: A Comparative Study of Informal Networks in Egypt, Iran and Lebanon;* Gause's chapter on "Representation and Participation" in his *Oil Monarchies: Domestic and Security Challenges in the Arab Gulf States,* pp. 78–118; Ghabra, "Voluntary Associations in Kuwait: The Foundation of a New System"; Hiltermann, *Behind the Intifada: Labor and Women's Movements in the Occupied Territories;* Lawson, *Oppositional Movements and U.S. Policy Toward the Arab Gulf States;* Singerman, *Avenues of Participation: Family, Politics, and Networks in Urban Quarters of Cairo;* Sullivan, *Private Voluntary Organizations in Egypt: Islamic Development, Private Initiative, and State Control;* and White, *Money Makes Us Relatives: Women's Labor in Urban Turkey.* Dozens of additional studies are cited in the bibliography.

40. Springborg, *Western Republicanism,* p. 20, citing Rostovtzeff, *Caravan Cities.*

41. See Goldberg, "Private Goods, Public Wrongs, and Civil Society in Some Medieval Arab Theory and Practice."

42. Bellin, "Civil Society: Effective Tool of Analysis for Middle East Politics?" p. 509. In addition to the citations in this chapter, dozens of books and articles on civil society by scholars, both inside and outside of the Middle East, are cited in this volume's multi-language bibliography.

43. See Norton, Introduction to *Civil Society in the Middle East,* vol. 1.

44. Norton, "The Future of Civil Society in the Middle East," p. 211.

45. Norton draws on O'Donnell and Schmitter, *Transitions from Authoritarian Rule: Tentative Conclusions About Uncertain Democracies;* Putnam, *Making Democracy Work: Civic Traditions in Modern Italy;* and Edward Shils, "The Virtue of Civil Society," among others.

46. Bellin, "Civil Society: Effective Tool of Analysis for Middle East Politics?" p. 509.

47. Norton, "The Future of Civil Society," pp. 213–214.

48. Norton, Introduction to *Civil Society in the Middle East,* vol. 1, p. 11.

49. Chazan, "Africa's Democratic Challenge," p. 283 (emphasis added).

50. See Hicks and al-Najjar, "Civil Society in Kuwait" (summary included in this volume); and Ghabra, "Voluntary Association in Kuwait: The Foundations of a New System?"

51. For example, see Diamond, "Three Paradoxes of Democracy."

52. See Entelis, "Civil Society and the Authoritarian Temptation in Algerian Politics: Islamic Democracy vs. the Centralized State"; and Maghraoui, "Algeria's Short-Lived Experiment with Electoral Politics" (summaries included in this volume.)

53. See Kazemi and Norton, *Civil Society and the Prospects for Political Reform in the Middle East* (summary included in this volume).

54. Ibrahim, "Crises, Elites, and Democratization in the Arab World," p. 304 (summary included in this volume).

55. Ibid., pp. 292–294.

56. See the collection of essays in Boulding, *Building Peace in the Middle East: Challenges for States and Civil Society.*

57. The term "Islamist" is used in this chapter to refer to organizations or individuals that find mandate for political and social reorganization in the teachings of Islamic texts and sources, including the Qur'an, the *Hadith* (pl. *Huwadith*) or teachings of the Prophet Muhammad, and individual Muslim thinkers throughout history. "Islamism" is often referred to elsewhere as "Islamic fundamentalism" or "political Islam."

58. For example, one reason Hizbollah faired well in the 1992 parliamentary

elections in Lebanon was their history of providing basic social services to war-torn South Lebanon. See Norton and Schwedler, "Swiss Soldiers, Ta'if Clocks, and Early Elections: Toward a Happy Ending in Lebanon?" For a look at services provided by Islamist groups in Egypt, see Sullivan, *Private Voluntary Organizations in Egypt.*

59. Kedourie, *Democracy and Arab Political Culture,* p. 1.

60. See Ahmed, *Postmodernism and Islam: Predicament and Promise;* Esposito and Piscatori, "Democratization and Islam"; and Krämer, "Liberalization and Democracy in the Arab World."

61. See Esposito, *The Islamic Threat: Myth or Reality?* and Hadar, "What Green Peril?"

62. See Norton, *Introduction to Civil Society in the Middle East,* vol. 1; and Moussalli, "Modern Islamic Fundamentalist Discourses on Civil Society, Pluralism, and Democracy" (summary included in this volume). Also see Esposito, *The Islamic Threat: Myth or Reality?* and Esposito and Piscatori, "Democratization and Islam."

63. See Kazemi and Norton, *Civil Society and the Prospects for Political Reform in the Middle East.*

64. Asad, "Religion and Politics: An Introduction," p. 9.

65. Rosefsky-Wickham, "Beyond Democratization: Political Change in the Arab World," p. 508.

66. See Brand, "'In the Beginning Was the State . . .' Civil Society in Jordan," and Carapico, "Yemen Between Civility and Civil War" (summaries included in this volume); and Norton and Schwedler, "Swiss Soldiers, Ta'if Clocks, and Early Elections: Toward a Happy Ending in Lebanon?"

67. Hudson, "Democratization and the Problem of Legitimacy in Middle East Politics," p. 168.

68. See Woods, "Civil Society in Europe and Africa: Limiting State Power Through a Public Sphere."

69. Habermas, *The Structural Transformation,* p. 85.

70. Weiner, "Retrieving Civil Society in a Postmodern Epoch"; and Habermas, *Theory of Communicative Action,* vol. 2, pp. 536–539.

71. Seligman, *The Idea of Civil Society,* p. 6.

72. Ibid., p. 5.

73. Ibid., p. 27. For an account of how the ideas of "reason" and "civil society" came to be "sacralized" in Europe during the Enlightenment, see Jacob, "Private Beliefs in Public Temples: The New Religiosity of the Eighteenth Century."

74. See Mardin, "Civil Society: A Comparative Approach" (under revision for publication). Cited with the kind permission of the author.

75. Ibid., p. 4.

76. Ibid., p. 12.

77. The forces perceived as guiding Islamic societies vary among sects: following the prophet Muhammad's death in 632 A.D., the Sunnis institutionalized Muhammad's charismatic authority in the caliphate, and the Shi'as perpetuated his charisma through the identification of an Imam. See Dabashi, *Authority in Islam.*

78. A similar argument is made by Gellner in his *Conditions of Liberty: Civil Society and Its Rivals.*

79. Bromley, *Rethinking Middle East Politics,* especially pp. 16–18.

80. Ibid.

81. See Batatu, *The Old Social Classes and the Revolutionary Movements of Iraq.*

82. Springborg, *Western Republicanism,* p. 20, citing Rostovzeff, *Caravan Cities.*

83. See Goldberg, "Private Goods, Public Wrongs, and Civil Society in Some Medieval Arab Theory and Practice."

84. Shils, "The Virtue of Civil Society," p. 15.

85. Ibid.

86. Keane, Introduction to *Civil Society and the State,* pp. 1–31.

87. Shils, "The Virtue of Civil Society," p. 4.

88. Gellner, *Conditions of Liberty: Civil Society and Its Rivals,* p. 184.

89. Ibid., p. 189.

90. O'Donnell and Schmitter, *Tentative Conclusions About Uncertain Democracies,* p. 48.

91. Ibid., p. 49.

92. Norton, "The Future of Civil Society," pp. 211 and 212, respectively.

93. Ibid., p. 215. Also see Keane, *Democracy and Civil Society,* p. 23; and Diamond, "Rethinking Civil Society," pp. 4–17.

94. Norton, Introduction to *Civil Society in the Middle East,* vol. 1, p. 11.

95. This idea—that the institutionalization of legal protection for certain fundamental human rights may facilitate the emergence of civil society—is different from the modernization theory, which posits that liberal democracy will emerge as a "traditional" society passes certain thresholds of economic, social, and political development. The idea that all countries should or must follow a prescribed course of development in order to modernize and advance has been largely, but not entirely, abandoned. For one of the classic works of liberal modernization theory, see Huntington, *Political Order in Changing Societies.* Also see Huber, Rueschemeyer, and Stephens, "The Impact of Economic Development on Democracy," who argue that there is a causal relation between the level of economic development and the development of political democracy (p. 83)—especially with regard to the shift in the balance of class power—but not one that is "unilinear or automatic" (p. 75).

96. Hudson, "Democratization and the Problem of Legitimacy in Middle East Politics," p. 169.

97. Melucci, "The Symbolic Challenge of Contemporary Movements," p. 790.

98. See Gause's observation in his "Sovereignty, Statecraft, and Stability in the Middle East," that foreign policy in the Middle East has revolved largely around questions of sovereignty and attempts to redraw state boundaries within the region. In this light, a state's posture of tolerance and civility toward challenges from its own citizens must be viewed with caution, and perhaps even a degree of skepticism.

99. See Brand, "'In the Beginning Was the State . . .' Civil Society in Jordan" (summary included in this volume); and Wedeman, "Democracy in Jordan."

100. See Hinnebusch, "State, Civil Society and Political Change in Syria," and al-Sayyid, "A Civil Society in Egypt?" (summaries included in this volume); and Zubaida, "Islam, the State, and Democracy: Contrasting Conceptions of Society in Egypt."

101. Rosefsky-Wickham, "Beyond Democratization: Political Change in the Arab World," p. 508.

102. Seligman, *The Idea of Civil Society,* p. 31.

103. Mitchell, "The Limits of the State," p. 78.

104. Ibid.

105. O'Donnell and Schmitter, *Tentative Conclusions About Uncertain Democracies,* p. 49.

106. Melucci, "The Symbolic Challenge of Contemporary Movements," p. 793.

107. Rosefsky-Wickham argues in her "Beyond Democratization: Political Change in the Arab World," that the political change under way in the Arab world in general, and Egypt in particular, cannot be accurately described as the development of an independent civil society. In fact, "efforts to locate civil society or other 'prerequisites' of democratic reform reveal more about the preoccupations of Western scholars than they do about new social configurations in the Middle East today" (p. 509).

108. Asad, "Religion and Politics: An Introduction," p. 11.

109. Also see Migdal, *Strong Societies and Weak States.*

110. Norton, Introduction to *Civil Society in the Middle East,* vol. 1, p. 11.

111. Several scholars have argued that the conventional dichotomy between the state and civil society is problematic even as an ideal type. See Offe, "New Social Movements: Challenging the Boundaries of Institutional Politics"; and Misztal and Misztal, "Democratization Processes as an Objective of New Social Movements."

Summaries of Individual Studies

The following collection of country studies and thematic papers examines civil society in the Middle East. The authors approach their topics from different perspectives and disciplines, providing a rich array of analyses that probe the existence and viability of civil society under varying conditions. If the authors agree on one issue, it is that civil society cannot flourish when a government's aim is to control or restrict associational activity. This may seem obvious. Yet, the lesson magnified is that although a civil society may foster tolerance, it is the state that provides space in which associations can function openly. When the state resorts to repression, social forces will have no alternative but to act outside the boundaries of the civil society and government control.

Many of the studies in this book appear as full-length chapters in the two-volume set on *Civil Society in the Middle East,* edited by Augustus Richard Norton. Several additional studies, presented at project-sponsored conferences or published by project personnel, have been included here to illustrate the wide range of issues that may be explored through the study of civil society. (Full citations for all contributions appear in the Bibliography.)

1

The Future of Civil Society in the Middle East

Augustus Richard Norton

The new language of Middle East politics stresses participation, cultural authenticity, freedom, and even democracy. Middle Eastern governments continue to suffer eroding legitimacy, even as they feel increasing pressure from their citizens. Although there is no doubt the political elite intend to stay in power, the imperative of political reform is widely felt in ruling circles. Nonetheless, while some rulers has been willing to liberalize, none has been willing to comprehensively democratize, although they often ply a democratic vocabulary to win international favor.

Liberalization refers to reformist measures to open up outlets for the free expression of opinion, to place limits on the arbitrary exercise of power, and to permit political association. In contrast, democratization—freely contested elections—has only been timidly attempted. The prevailing ideology of opposition is Islamism. Many of the region's Islamist movements espouse free elections and political reform, but some Islamists are contemptuous, even hostile toward democracy and many thoughtful Middle Easterners justifiably fear Islamist totalitarianism. However, the Islamists are only one component in civil society. The argument here is that the emergence of civil society is a crucial step toward realizing a freer Middle East.

The symbol of democracy is the contested election via the secret ballot, but the home of democracy is in civil society, where a mélange of groups, associations, and clubs provide a buffer between state and citizen. The existence of a civil society implies a shared sense of identity and a sense of citizenship, with associated rights and responsibilities, which autocracies promote but tend to trivialize. The underpinning value of civil society is civility, the willingness of individuals to accept disparate political views and social attitudes; to accept the profoundly important idea that there is no right answer. In the Middle East, civil society is often undermined by a deficit in political toleration and constricted by arbitrary government regulation.

Although elements of civil society are likely to oppose the government, it is naive to expect civil society to topple the state. The goal of civil society is reform, not revolution. Reform will follow many paths. In some cases, rulers will adopt what the Arabs call "facade democracy," employing the vocabulary of democracy while proceeding with business as usual. But the pressures to open up the political systems may not abate. As civil society continues to gain its footing, issues of accountability and performance will grow in importance. Although regular encroachments upon the dignity of individuals linger, the trajectory of Middle East politics is clearly toward an increased emphasis on individual rights to be free from the arbitrary abuse of the state.

From "The Future of Civil Society in the Middle East," *Middle East Journal,* Spring 1993

2

Modern Islamic Fundamentalist Discourses on Civil Society, Pluralism, and Democracy

Ahmad Moussalli

The record on Islamic fundamentalist attitudes toward civil society needs to be set straight. Islamic fundamentalism is not a monolithic bloc, but includes a variety of discourses on the relationship between the individual, society, and the state. In the theoretical foundations of civil society developed under different Islamic regimes, two main schools of thought emerge concerning the viability and necessity of civil society in Islam. On the one hand, a limited number of radical fundamentalists look negatively at strengthening civil society. On the other hand, moderate fundamentalists, who compose the significant majority of fundamentalist thinkers, call for establishing pluralistic civil society as the cornerstone of the new Islamic state. In fact, claim the moderates, civil society is precisely Islam's original and ideal form of society. In addition, a theoretical assessment of fundamentalist positions on civil society and democracy reveals Islamists are actively engaged in discussing both the possibility of grounding Islamic and Western political thought in a universal framework, and the potential for peaceful coexistence between Islamic and Western societies. Given these current debates, the question is whether a cultural clash between the East and West is inevitable.

The early existence of civil society in Muslim societies reveals that many civil groups flourished, including the craft's brotherhoods, Sufi orders, the notables, *'ulama* circles and minorities' institutions. The Sufi orders were connected with the crafts, and the notables reflected the rights of civil institutions to conduct affairs autonomous from the state. These civil groups created a multilayered framework through which individuals organized in each community and they connected this framework to the more general ideal of the Islamic community.

Islamic fundamentalism is not a theoretically and politically unified movement. However, certain terms and concerns are common to all debates, including the supremacy of *tawhid* as the pivotal doctrinal and political foundation, the superiority of the *shari'ah,* and the establishment of an Islamic state. Two major discourses are discernible, especially with regard to civil society.

First, there is the discourse of a radical trend grounded in a few exclusivist concepts: authenticity, one-sidedness of the truth, purity, superiority, and, above all, salvational knowledge. The main theoreticians and adherents of these concepts, such as Sayyid Qutb, Salih Sirriyyah, Mustapha Shukri, and 'Umar 'Abd al-Rahman, tend to be self-righteous and undemocratic. They believe a properly conducted *shura* creates a social or public will that is more important than the individual or the group that must submit to it. In an Islamic system, this public will represents the divine will. Therefore, individuals or groups cannot legitimately stand in opposition. For these radicals, individual freedom is secondary to the interest of the community. No parties or associations are allowed to tamper with political or even social unity. Insofar as the government is not disobeying the divine law, it cannot be legitimately toppled. Such an environment is, of course, not conducive to the establishment of pluralist civil societies or the flourishing of freedom.

The second trend, moderate fundamentalism, allows pluralistic interpretations based on the simple idea that no man can produce a final interpretative judgment. Legislative processes must reflect a society's beliefs and interests. Moderate thinkers, including Hasan al-Banna, Rashid al-Ghannushi, and Hasan al-Turabi, attribute violence to the absence of democratic institutions and pluralistic civil societies. They see no contradiction between Islam and Western philosophies and institutions. The moderates can bridge the East-West cultural gap, deny exclusivity of Islamic thought, and attribute East-West conflicts to historical political factors by insisting these systems and institutions, when properly grounded, are truly Islamic.

Since the East and West have common religious and philosophical roots, ample room exists for multicultural religious cooperation and coexistence.

3

Democratization in the Arab World

Saad Eddin Ibrahim

Much of the literature circulating on the transition from nondemocratic to democratic rule finds a fertile testing ground in the Arab world. While belonging to one general political-cultural area, the twenty-one Arab countries offer global factors associated with such transitions—for example, nature and evolution of the state, political regimes, class structure, political culture, levels of socioeconomic development, and civil society. Yet, despite its particularities, the Arab world is evolving along the same broad trends and processes that have been at work elsewhere in newly democratizing societies.

Four variables—socioeconomic formations, the articulation of civil society, the state, and external factors—have been acting upon each other to produce a mini-wave of democratization in the Arab world. The interplay varies from one Arab country to another, which accounts for the degree of democratization empirically observed in each at present.

Civil society in the Arab world has revitalized itself in the last two decades due to internal, regional, and international factors. Internally, new socioeconomic formations that the autocratic and/or populist regimes have no longer been able to accommodate or completely suppress have been growing steadily. Regionally, protracted armed conflicts have weakened the state, exposed its impotence in managing such conflicts, and drained its resources. Meanwhile, other regional developments have unwittingly empowered new and old constituencies within each Arab state. Internationally, the patron-client relationship between Arab regimes and the two superpowers has either ended or been greatly altered. The global wave of democratization has also had its marked demonstration effect on the expanding Arab middle class.

Sprouting civil society organizations in the Arab world have pressured for greater liberalization to atone for the state's failure in meeting socioeconomic needs by tending to itself and, later, for its reluctance to respond to their political quest for participation. The sluggish performance of the state vis-à-vis these demands has led many disenfranchised youngsters of the lower middle class to espouse Islamic militancy as a mode of protest.

During the 1980s and early 1990s, the Arab world has witnessed a three-way race to maintain or seize power among autocratic regimes, Islamic activists, and civil society organizations. In some Arab countries, one variant of the race has been the squeezing of civil society out of the public arena by autocratic regimes and Islamic activists. In another variant, both the autocratic regimes and Islamic activists have attempted to win over or appropriate civil society organizations.

This second variant contains the greatest promise for civil society and, hence, for the democratization process. Importantly, it has provided ample bargaining power to civil society organizations when they deal with the state in attempts to gain concessions of the sociopolitical reformative nature. It also has had a moderating effect on several Islamic activist groups. In Jordan, Kuwait, Yemen, and Lebanon this promise has actually been unfolding. In all four, Islamists have accepted the principle of political pluralism, participating alongside other secular forces in national elections. Islamists are currently represented in those countries' parliaments. In Lebanon, Yemen, and Jordan women have been elected for the first time, and the Islamists did not march out in protest.

So long as religious-based parties and associations accept the principle of pluralism and observe a modicum of civility in behavior toward the different "other," then they can expect to be integral parts of civil society. In this respect, even the Islamists may evolve into something akin to the Christian Democrats in the West or the religious parties in Israel. There is nothing intrinsically Islamic that contradicts with the codes of civil society or democratic principles.

The responses by Arab regimes to their civil societies indicate as many prospects for further democratization as against it. The modernizing monarchies, namely of Jordan and Morocco, have impressively engineered a smooth transition toward more democratic governance. Their example may tilt the balance toward greater democratic prospects in the entire region; prospects that promise to enhance the peaceful settlement of some of the region's protracted conflicts while also growing in strength from such settlements.

4

Economic Pressures for Accountable Governance in the Middle East and North Africa

Alan Richards

Can democracy find a home in the Middle East? Neo-Orientalists assert that the absence of traditional civil society, the weakness of the middle classes, and Islamic conceptions of the state all doom any hope of the region's participating in the current worldwide upsurge of democratic politics. Still, while few would predict a major thrust toward democracy in the late twentieth-century Middle East, the glimmerings of civil society undeniably glow rather more brightly in the region these days.

In fact, economic imperatives dictate heightened political participation in the region. For most of the period since the nations of the Middle East gained independence, industrial technologies and development strategies favored centralization and autocracy. Today, the opposite is true. The legacy of past decades will not be easily overcome. However, in the modern international economy of information technologies, discriminating consumers, and intense competition, only economies less centralized than those of the Arab world will survive. Increasingly, national leaders recognize the necessity of change—structural adjustment and economic liberalization are on the agenda of nearly all regional states—and will require increased political participation in some form. Coping with the challenges surrounding food, jobs, and investment will require greater integration into the international economy; such economic changes imply enlarging the role of the private sector, widening the scope of the rule of law, and more generally restructuring the state's relations with its citizens.

Still, economic forces do not make democratization inevitable. There are always choices in politics, but these choices are constrained for the simple reason that if economic challenges are not met, sociopolitical problems accumulate and the range of choices narrows accordingly. In particular, old-style "Arab socialist" options are no longer viable. If rulers want to survive, they will be forced to make some concessions to economic logic. Such concessions can only be avoided if a regime has a dependable source of income, which generates few political demands upon acquisition. Although oil-rents provided such politically easy money in the past, they shrank markedly during the middle and late 1980s, and the prospects for future oil prices are uncertain. The choice has narrowed to the stark one between accommodation to economic reality (which has political implications) or a descent into chaos.

Let us be clear: Just because solving (or even ameliorating) mounting economic problems requires wider political participation does not mean that it will happen. Failure is possible, even likely for many countries. Auto-economic suicide is a real alternative; challenges may not be met, and explosions are real dangers. Lebanon, Bosnia, and Somalia represent all-too-vivid alternatives to economic progress, as do the continuing famines in the Sudan. Economic determinism will serve us poorly. But equally, ignoring economic forces will deceive us as to the consequences of policy choices.

The task will not be easy. The natural resource base, with its mix of abundant oil and scarce water, makes adjustment imperative, but also makes it difficult. Habits will die hard—entrenched interest groups, engendered over nearly a half-century of state centralization, will not be easily persuaded to abandon their privileges. For the governments, there are really only two alternatives: repression or participation. Repression is likely to be ineffective in the long run, and it impedes constructing the institutions that afford an opportunity for coping with the economic challenges of the immediate future.

Expanded participation need not mean "democracy" in the current Western sense. Middle Eastern nations will doubtless have to find their own culturally authentic paths to expanded participation. Whatever the precise forms, expanded participation will be essential for three reasons. First, the age of structural adjustment is the age of subsidy cuts. Economically, a subsidy cut is equivalent to a tax increase. Political participation is necessary to "share the pain." Second, a stable legal environment is a necessary condition for a functioning market economy. Since there are no alternatives to markets for many allocative purposes, the only alternative to the rule of law is economic stagnation, poverty, and, ultimately, chaos. Third, properly functioning markets require widely available modern information technology as well as secure property rights. But the faxes that carry this morning's price data also may convey the latest statement of the exiled political opposition. If a regime simply outlaws the use of fax machines outside of its control (as does Syria), it will not be able to effectively compete in international markets. Accordingly, it cannot solve the problems associated with food, jobs, and money.

Consequently, Middle Eastern governments have much adjusting to do if they hope to cope with the economic imperatives of the last decade of the twentieth century. They will need to privatize and acquiesce to their own laws, assist their private exporters in foreign markets, and educate their young, among other things. Some countries may rise to the challenge; some will likely fail. The costs of failure will be very high and will affect not only their own people and their neighbors but also the international community. The alternative road of repression, civil war, economic stagnation, food insecurity, poverty, and chaos is all too familiar to people of the region. However, the fact there is an "economic imperative" does not mean politics will rise to the occasion. But the stark choice—participation or repression—will be faced by policymakers both within and without the region.

5

Civil Society and the Authoritarian Temptation in Algerian Politics

John P. Entelis

In the Middle East, one of the most "successful" examples of the bureau-cratic-authoritarian state has been postindependence Algeria. Fueled by impressive hydrocarbon resources, a revolutionary elite attempted to trans-form a backward, agricultural society into a modern, industrialized state through a highly centralized system of command and control. In a sort of "ruling bargain," the Algerian people traded their right to organize political-ly for public social welfare.

The Algerian technocratic state of the 1970s illustrated how autonomous development could take place without intervention from domestic social forces or their global collaborators. By the mid-1980s, how-ever, when world oil and natural gas prices declined and massive industrial projects faltered or collapsed altogether, the ruling bargain had become unstuck as the economic conditions that financed this arrangement began to disintegrate.

The depth of the failure was evidenced by the nationwide riots of October 1988, when autonomous social forces emerged with incredible vigor to challenge the hegemony of state power. Workers, farmers, students, street people, Islamic militants, feminists, and Berberists rose to violently protest their continued marginality and subordination. Algeria could no more escape the "infection" of society-based "revolution" than its ideologi-cal counterparts in Eastern Europe. Indeed, the "expanding society, retreat-ing state" rubric seemed the more appropriate designation for the Algeria of the 1990s. Yet, the return of army rule to Algeria in early 1992 demonstrat-ed the fragility of civil society and the durability of political authoritarian-ism.

Has the Algerian state exhausted its current democratic phase, moved into a period of temporary stock taking in preparation for a further democratic advance, or retreated to its authoritarian past? Although the traditional institutions of power—the military-industrial complex, ex–National Liberation Front (FLN) hard-liners, the government bureaucracy—have reasserted their power, an array of social forces continues to vocalize discontent, from the five hundred thousand–strong demonstration of Socialist Forces Front (FFS) supporters in December 1990 to fundamentalist grievances against secular policies. Trying to break the paralysis of fear, those now in power find themselves afraid of the consequences. Government officials warn against collapse to justify maintaining the state of siege.

Islamic appeals in Algeria have responded to socioeconomic grievances and cultural demands for integrity, authenticity, and identity. In their dualistic messages, the Islamic Salvation Front (FIS) formulated a legitimate political discourse consistent with Algerian culture, history, and experience. Yet, no meaningful democracy can emerge that does not first have popular sovereignty founded on a collective national identity, shared historic vision, and common cultural values. Although this paradox of democratization has proven difficult to resolve, the alternative is to overturn the basic democratic principle of full participation. Nowhere in the Arab world has a multiparty election in a formerly one-party state directly replaced a party in power. The ultimate test of democracy's "true" effect, therefore, will be when such a turnover takes place. This also will reveal the "true" measure of the autonomy of civil society.

From *Civil Society in the Middle East,* vol. 2

6

Algeria's Short-Lived Experiment with Electoral Politics

Abdeslam Maghraoui

Algeria was the first Arab country to be genuinely involved in a serious and promising experiment with multiparty democracy. The evolving political events in Algeria concern Middle East specialists because they reflect the dilemma of democratization in many Muslim societies where Islamic groups constitute a powerful political force. A strong belief exists that a similar scenario could unfold in other Arab states, including Egypt, Jordan, Tunisia, and Lebanon as well as in the West Bank and the Gaza Strip. Political analysts disagree considerably on what to make of the short-lived Algerian democratic test. Three main propositions have emerged to explain the debacle: the poor management skills of the reformer teams; the lack of a credible and well-organized secular alternative; and a deep crisis within Islamic societies vainly in quest for a "utopian polis."

These perspectives all violate some basic liberal democratic principles. This necessarily applies to both those who rationalize the interruption of the democratic process where Muslim fundamentalists are the obvious winners, and to those who make the case for maintaining the democratic process regardless of the political outcome. The former pays no attention to the question of popular sovereignty, without which democracy is meaningless if not impossible. The latter reduces democracy to the formal act of organizing free elections with no consideration for individual rights.

A third approach holds that the Islamists' political project is essentially in harmony with some basic democratic principles, but is inconsistent with fundamental liberal values and ideals. This dichotomy is best understood as a conflict within liberal democratic theory, which Islamic fundamentalism inadvertently brings to the open. This new outlook will force us to radically restructure our understanding of the region's democratic paradox. More specifically, if the problem with an "Islamic democracy" is the inherent dichotomy between the obligations of the citizen toward a community—

44

defined on religious principles—and the rights of the citizen as an individual, it is within Islamic discursive conventions that the solution will arise.

The popularity of the Islamic parties in Algeria is not simply a response to immediate economic problems, political frustrations, or social injustice. It is *equally* an effort to define what is a good polity and achieve popular sovereignty on the basis of Islamic traditions. If we examine the resurgence and politicization of Islamic sentiments in Algeria from this perspective, we will realize that what is happening there is not much different from the resurgence of nationalism in Eastern Europe and the former Soviet Union. People everywhere are struggling to achieve sovereignty by making a fundamental demand: recognition of their ethnic, linguistic, or religious identities. However, these popular and legitimate demands are potentially subversive to liberal democracy.

The Islamic leaders are not concerned that their political project is incompatible with secular liberal democracy. What should concern them, however, is the argument made by an increasing number of Muslims that the fundamentalists' political agenda violates some basic Islamic principles. If the FIS's theocratic state subverts basic democratic principles, subsumed in Islamic sources, precedents, and political philosophy, then it is incumbent on Muslims to challenge the Islamic leaders on the basis of Islamic discursive conventions.

Religion will continue to shape the political landscape of the Middle East, and internal pressures to democratize will only increase. There are no magic solutions or universal formulas for peacefully reconciling religious demands with democratic principles. Cultural traditions vary and so will the solutions. It would be naive to expect democratic development in the Middle East without an Islamic imprint.

From "Algeria's Short-lived Experiment with Electoral Politics," *Middle East Insight,* July–October 1993

7

A Civil Society in Egypt?

Mustapha Kamil al-Sayyid

Intellectual debates over the uses and abuses of civil society have been echoing in the Arab world. The controversy was triggered by the democratic wave that hit the shores of authoritarianism in Eastern and Southern Europe, and Southern Asia. Some Arab intellectuals believed they also saw signs of the resurgence of civil society in the Arab world.

While intellectuals debated theoretical propositions, a substantive transformation in social processes was under way in Egypt, Jordan, Kuwait, Lebanon, Mauritania, Morocco, Tunisia, and Yemen (as well as Algeria prior to the military coup in late December 1991). Many contradictory features were noticeable, particularly in Egypt. On the one hand, divisive social groups were gaining more freedom to express dissenting views in professional associations and in political parties. On the other hand, individuals claiming to act in the name of Islamist organizations were effectively challenging the government, and not only in the remote villages of Upper Egypt. In Cairo, for example, Islamists' attacks against Copts, foreign tourists, and individuals voicing opposition to their mission have reached alarming proportions since the summer of 1992. Victims include Farag Fouda, Egypt's most famous secularist writer, in June 1992, and an American and a French law professor during President Hosni Mubarak's visit to the United States and France in October 1993. In addition to those assassinations, attacks were made on the ministers of information (April 1993) and the interior (August 1993), both of whom were wounded, and the prime minister (25 November 1993), who was not harmed in the attempt on his life. Moreover, many usually moderate voices of the Islamist movement branded intellectuals critical of their views apostates. The sentence for apostasy, which Islamists believe to be sanctioned by *shari'ah,* is death. In the event the government fails to carry out that sentence, the punishment may be imposed by any Muslim.

While the state has permitted a degree of autonomy for societal actors, some of them, ironically, have demonstrated intolerance for the exercise of freedom of speech, worship, and action by others. Herein lies the contradiction: If associational autonomy is definitely a measure of the resurgence of a civil society, acts of intolerance cast doubts on its "civil" character. These contradictory tendencies warrant an examination of the extent to which civil society exists in Egypt and the factors likely to affect its evolution.

Unfortunately, the prospects for civil society in Egypt seem to have deteriorated in recent years. Egypt, together with their supporters in the United States and international financial institutions, must realize economic liberalism does not offer a panacea for dealing with diverse economic and social problems in developing countries. Without that realization, government-imposed limitations on civil society will increase, and the bloody confrontation between security forces and young impoverished Egyptians who believe they are fighting for an Islamic cause will widen, bringing protracted chaos to Egypt's embryonic civil society.

From *Civil Society in the Middle East,* vol. 1

8

Civil Society and Iranian Politics

Farhad Kazemi

In the Islamic Republic of Iran, civil society may be understood as the space where a plethora of groups, associations, and organizations have operated outside the immediate domain of the state. Major problems confronting civil society in Iran have been the increasing power of the state, its autonomy, and the attempt by the state to control civil society. This process began in the nineteenth century with the Qajar dynasty's attempts at military modernization in response to defeats on the war front. Modernization soon spread to other areas and resulted in perceptively increasing power of the Iranian state over its citizens. With the emergence of the Pahlavi dynasty in 1925, centralization of state power continued, helped considerably by the establishment, for the first time, of a standing national army based on universal male conscription. During the last phase of the Pahlavi dynasty, and with its increased dependence on oil rent, state power and its autonomy from the pressures of civil society reached a new height.

With final victory of the Islamic revolution in 1979, and in spite of some initial signals to the contrary, the process of domination of the state over social, economic, and political affairs became apparent. The theocratic vision of the Islamic Republic of Iran has added an important new dimension to the state's role by defining citizenship rights (and civility) in essentially rigid religious terms. This has resulted in a strong communitarian view with clear notions of inclusion and exclusion of subjects in the polity. It also has led to justifications and rationalizations for intermittent abuses of individual rights. Two groups in particular have suffered the most from this development—religious minorities and women. Of special relevance here is the situation of the nonrecognized Baha'is and the change in the criminal code with its deleterious effect on women's legal status.

Even with these restrictions, many semiautonomous groups, associations, and organizations have been able to function outside immediate state control. Most important among these include the multifaceted foundations *(bonyads)* which are divided into three categories of public, private, and

Islamic charitable foundations *(awqaf).* Private foundations are less significant than the other two. Among public foundations, the Foundation for the
Oppressed and the Martyr's Foundation stand out for their importance in the
social order and as the indirect arms of the government. Due to their wealth
and resources and their extensive patron-client ties with the population at
large, these and other foundations have some potential for challenging state
dominance in the future. Pressure on the government may come more clearly from a host of guilds, Islamic committees, and professional associations
that have provided some degree of separateness from the state. Although
their collective importance remains to be seen, they are a significant expression of civil society in Iran. Therefore, in spite of the state's attempt to dominate and control, civil society in Iran remains viable and continues to function and even expand its base.

9

Civil Society Under the Ba'th in Iraq

Zuhair Humadi

Modern Iraqi history can be divided into three periods: the monarchy (1921–1958), the rule of the military (1958–1968), and the Ba'th rule (1968–present).

The constitutional monarchy, which followed the British mandate, had undeniably democratic characteristics. The composition of the bicameral parliament reflected the diversity of the Iraqi population, and its upper chamber, which consisted of appointed members, included prominent representatives of the political opposition. Governments were answerable to the parliament and were afforded significant freedoms.

Although many organizations (such as the Iraqi Communist Party) were outlawed, and some ethnic groups, especially the Assyrians, were harshly persecuted, a degree of criticism was tolerated. Issues of public interest were openly debated in parliament and in the press and were often critical of the government; as a result, instances of political protest were common. This climate of relative openness, combined with the free trade economy, enabled civil society to flourish. For example, the Baghdad Chamber of Commerce was an active participant in the country's economy. The Iraqi Bar Association also exercised considerable societal influence—for example, a section of the association's organization was mandated to defend civil liberties, fulfilling a role similar to that of the ACLU in the United States. Associations of intellectuals openly voiced their opinions. In view of what was to follow, this period should be considered civil society's golden era in Iraq.

If the monarchy was civil society's golden era in Iraq, the subsequent decade of military rule was a period of transition from relative openness to dictatorship. This era was ushered in by a bloody coup and was characterized by an unprecedented level of violent action by political parties, in particular by the Communists during Qassim's premiership and the Ba'thists during the ten months that followed. In several respects the military rule served as a precursor to the rule of the Ba'th. For example, the war with the

Kurds began in this period and the nationalization of private enterprise was initiated. In general, the application became more arbitrary. However, apolitical institutions remained generally unaffected and continued to participate in public life.

In 1968, the Ba'th Party took power in a bloodless coup, but their true nature was revealed in the public hangings that followed their ascent to leadership. The Ba'thists embarked on a systematic campaign to impose their totalitarian ideology, gradually taking control of the government, the armed forces, and all aspects of public and associational life; echoing the communist takeovers throughout Eastern Europe. Even traditional organizations, such as religious institutions, were placed under the party's sphere of influence. During the earlier period of military rule the state had constricted private enterprise; the Ba'thists sought to weaken the private sector further by making foreign trade a government monopoly. Private and parochial schools were nationalized and school curricula were redefined, and free speech was dampened. The government even created a law requiring that all typewriters be "fingerprinted."

This government's absorption of public life was achieved through the systematic use of terror and enticement (*tarhib wa targhib*). Oil revenues provided enticement. Targets of state terrorism ranged from individuals to large segments of the population: chemical weapons were used against the Kurds; the areas inhabited by the Marsh Arabs of the South were dried up; membership, even suspected membership, in an outlawed political party was punished by death. Torture became a pervasive method of control. Not only those convicted for political offenses were persecuted, but punishment extended to the families of offenders (e.g., up to the fourth degree of kinship and all family members were excluded from the civil service). Since the government had become Iraq's largest employer, this particular punishment was a virtual sentence of poverty to the whole family.

Since 1979, when Saddam Hussein became president, the state and ruling party have become the entities in which there is no discussion, no collective bargaining, and no search for consensus on important issues. All issues are decided by the president, barring the possible involvement of a small circle of old-time associates and close family members, as the world witnessed in the onset of the Iran-Iraq war in 1980 and the invasion of Kuwait in 1990.

In short, civil society in Iraq was destroyed by the Ba'th's absolute control over all aspects of public and associational life in Iraq. For example, Iraqi doctors are now forced to brand foreheads and cut off the ears of army deserters, and amputate the hands or feet of petty thieves. Medical associations can only voice support for such measures.

This absolute control is not the only threat to Iraqi society. The destruction of the infrastructure during the Gulf War and, more important, the trade sanctions imposed by the UN following the invasion of Kuwait have exacerbated the disintegration of Iraqi society. The middle classes are pauperized, crime and petty theft are common, and public health hazards have reached alarming levels. Iraqis are finding it increasingly difficult to feed their families, as the currency has been rendered worthless by hyperinflation. Left without an alternative, many retreat to their tribal or ethnic roots, or seek refuge in individual religious practices.

Iraqi civil society cannot be revived so long as the Ba'th party remains in power, because of the Ba'th's inherently totalitarian ideology. In other words, a change of leadership, although necessary, will not be sufficient. The nature of the Iraqi state itself will have to be redefined, allowing the freedoms necessary for an embryonic civil society. This is the situation in the imposed safe haven north of the 36th Parallel, where, even though economic conditions are hardly better than elsewhere in Iraq and in spite of factional inter-Kurdish fighting, Iraqi citizens have begun to organize in a variety of independent associations. Sadly, Iraqi civil society is most vibrant outside Iraq. There are many examples of a growing civil society in the Iraqi diaspora, of which London, with its sizable Iraqi community, is the most important example. There, one can find many Iraqi cultural, religious, and professional organizations, and human rights advocacy groups, whose reach extends to Iraqis in many other parts of the world.

10

Two Civil Societies and One State: Jews and Arabs in the State of Israel

Gideon Doron

The Israeli regime exemplifies a case of nonliberal representative democracy. In it, two civil societies have evolved, and they are defined along religio-national lines. The larger contains mostly Jewish members; the smaller affects only the lives of the Arab citizens of Israel, who by 1992 constituted about 16 percent of the population. These two societies emerged roughly at the same time, about the mid-1970s, each with a distinct impetus to their respective development, scope, and internal characteristics. Thus, there is little spillover effect or interdependency between the two societies. The principle cause for the emergence of these two civil societies is the state's retreat from both its role as a caretaker of its Jewish majority, and its unwillingness to permit the Arabs to develop their own societal network.

The study of civil societies in the Middle East is based, among other things, on the analytical expectation that the growth in the scope of a civil society in a given country may generate conducive conditions for the development of democracy in that place. The principles underlying the idea of civil society—individual and group tolerance to opposing claims and interests, acceptance of one's own and others' modes of behavior and boundaries of identity, and voluntarism—also are seen as preconditions for the existence of vibrant democracy.

In this light, it may seem that because Israel is already a stable democracy, it cannot serve as a representative case for the study of the interrelation between the civil society and its regime, nor can one draw meaningful generalizations or policy inferences from its particular experience and compare it to the developmental process presently occurring in neighboring countries. The position advanced here, however, is that the study of the relationship between the state and the two emerging civil societies of Israel may be generalized to delineate those societies that, through a process of development, may evolve into nonliberal democracies. Thus, the relevancy of the study should be examined in places where the defining characteristic is the differential state attitude toward the constituent groups within its society. Other countries, both within and outside of the region, fall into this category.

The present emergence of the two civil societies in Israel is not a product of a normative design, nor is it a result of a consensual choice. Rather, the two societies are largely an outcome of default governance, and of domestic and international pressures to lift the control system that prevented the development of these societies, especially the Arab one. In this sense, the problems concerning the emergence of two civil societies in Israel may enhance our understanding of state-society relations and the emergence of liberal, participant governments in religiously or ethnically divided societies.

11

"In the Beginning Was the State . . ." Civil Society in Jordan

Laurie Brand

The Emirate of Transjordan was founded by the British as part of their imperial land-defense system in the Middle East. Poor in natural resources, the state was from its beginning heavily reliant upon external sources of budgetary support to enable it to play its assigned security role. The importance of the armed forces was further reinforced by the outbreak of the Arab-Israeli conflict in 1948, after which Jordan lived with the possibility war would break out anew with Israel.

The security role Jordan played for outside patrons over the years (depending upon period, Britain, the United States, or the Arab states) has significantly impacted civil society development in the country. In the first place, the long history of subsidies from abroad created an unusually large state sector. Second, the subsidies only served to reinforce the key role of security forces. Finally, the circumstances surrounding the annexation of part of Palestine (the East Bank) to the kingdom in 1950 meant the kingdom would rely primarily on one sector of its population, the native Transjordanians, for security and bureaucracy services. Hence, the state in effect appropriated about one-half of the population, the sector upon whose loyalty it felt it could count; the other community, the Palestinians, whose loyalty was viewed as questionable, was left to feel and be treated like second-class citizens. Such a situation contradicts one of the bases of a civil society—full citizenship for all citizens.

This is not to say civil society has been nonexistent in Jordan. Much activity was circumscribed by the long years of martial law, during which, for example, all political party activity was outlawed. However, a variety of professional associations and charitable societies were active during this period. In the absence of legal political party elections, the professional associations served as one of the few forums for gauging the political pulse of the country. Nonetheless, any activity that was seen as challenging the state was swiftly terminated.

This situation has begun to change since spring 1989. Economic crisis forced the king to begin a process of gradual and managed political liberalization. As a result, Jordan has witnessed two rounds of parliamentary elections, a legalization of political parties, greater freedom of the press (accompanied by a wave of new publications), the release of political prisoners, and vastly decreased harassment by the security forces. Jordan is also one of the only states in the Arab Middle East that has succeeded in incorporating the Islamists—who have a wide network of civil society institutions—into the political process.

These are all very encouraging signs. Nonetheless, the easing of authoritarianism's hold on civil society in Jordan is still quite new. The state's concern over the opposition to Jordan's peace agreement with Israel by the Islamists and other groups has led the state, on occasion, to constrict the realm of free expression and political activity. The prognosis for the further development of civil society is promising in Jordan. At this stage, however, the field of "battle" between the state and civil society in the kingdom remains overwhelmingly under the state's control.

12

Civil Society in Jordan: A Preliminary Study

Atef Odhibat

The Jordanian constitution grants King Hussein wide executive and legislative powers. However, it is his abilities, vision, and belief system that have contributed substantively to the emergence and activation of civil society and, as a result, the democratic transformation of Jordan. King Hussein has been gradually creating room for political participation since the early 1970s, when he established the Jordanian National Union, open to all Jordanians except the Communists and Marxists. The union was not a political party in the traditional sense, but more of a "melting pot for the Jordanian people." In 1978, a consultative council was created to study and debate legislative proposals. The group could submit recommendations and opinions to the King's cabinet, but their decisions were not binding.

Similar institutions were created over the years, offering gradually but steadily increasing space for political participation. Even during the years when partisan activities were banned, civil society organizations—that is, professional associations, trade unions, religious organizations, philanthropic groups, clubs, and community development groups—were permitted to function, express dissenting views, and lobby for reform.

This emergence and institutionalization of civil society in Jordan has served to both integrate and stabilize forces throughout the country, with no regional, communal, or partisan distinction. In fact, Jordanians, irrespective of their ethnic, religious, and ideological backgrounds, have been integrating around their major civil society organizations. The activities of civil society organizations in Jordan and the spirit of tolerance and coexistence prevailing among Jordanians have greatly contributed to the building of durable peace and stability within the country. This might explain why for the past two decades Jordan has been one of the most stable countries in the Arab world.

Still, Jordan faces two major challenges. First, women are underrepresented in civil society organizations; less than 10 percent of the total membership of professional associations in Jordan are women. Second, much of Jordanian civil society remains fragmented and does not form a united front vis-à-vis the state. Meeting these two challenges will determine the future of civil society in Jordan.

From an unpublished paper presented in Giza, Egypt, May 1992

13

Civil Society in Kuwait

Neil Hicks
Ghanim al-Najjar

Politics in Kuwait have been dominated by the ruling al-Sabah family since the country gained its independence from Britain in 1961, although family members ruled as emirs since 1952. Despite this tradition, the family has rarely been able to wield absolute authority. In order to put down a challenge from one part of society, the government has had to accommodate another. Thus, the institutions of civil society in Kuwait have developed in a political environment of controlled pluralism.

In the past, as oil revenues increased, so did the influence of the family. The Kuwaiti state took on primarily distributive functions and had no need to raise revenues from the population through taxation. Meanwhile, the government allowed opposition movements to organize and express their opinions within professional associations, religious groups, and cultural societies. However, the state maintained the power to suppress any group that went "too far" in its criticisms or demands.

Kuwait is unique among the monarchies of the Arabian Peninsula in having an established parliamentary tradition. Although the parliament is elected by only approximately 82,000 men, out of a Kuwaiti population in excess of 800,000, it has, through its thirty-year history, exhibited considerable independence.

From time to time, the government lost patience with this constraint on its authority and dissolved the parliament. The emir ruled by decree between 1976 and 1981, and between 1986 and 1992. However, the absence of the Assembly left the government with no outlet to obtain popular feedback on its policies.

With the National Assembly dissolved and formal associations under pressure, Kuwaitis turned to traditional home-based meetings, known as *diwaniyyat,* to voice their concerns. In the late 1980s, the *diwaniyyat,* beyond the legislative reach of the government, proved to be effective forums for campaigning for the restitution of the National Assembly, showing the modern relevance of a traditional institution.

The absence of the National Assembly and the polarization between the government and those calling for the reconvening of the Assembly, contributed to the policy mistakes that brought about the disaster of Iraqi occupation in August 1990. However, during the occupation and with the collapse of the government, the vibrancy of civil society sustained the Kuwaiti state. Leaders and activists from professional associations, religious associations, and the Cooperative Societies formed the backbone of popular resistance to the Iraqi occupation.

With the restoration of the emir in March 1991, the old government structures were reinstituted, but the balance of power changed with the ruling family much weakened by the invasion. Elections were held in October 1992 in which government supporters were defeated in thirty-six out of fifty seats. Nevertheless, the government maintains the whip because of its control of patronage and strong divisions within the opposition along ideological, tribal, class, and religious lines. The government continues to be torn between the temptation to exercise absolute power and the recognition that the popular consent necessary for stable rule comes from its accommodation of competing political interests with the society.

From *Civil Society in the Middle East,* vol. 1

14

Civil Society in
the Arab Gulf States

Jill Crystal

The received wisdom in much of the literature on the Middle East is that civil society in the Arab world has at best a fetal consciousness. Nowhere has this received wisdom been received more enthusiastically than in the study of the Gulf. Both the older literature, written from a dependency as well as modernization perspective, and much of the more recent literature on the rentier state conclude that independent groups are unimportant in the Gulf, that associational life is weak, and that the public space between the nuclear family and the state is sparsely populated.

To most writers, the historically important groups, the traditional groups, were bound to fade under the impact of modernization, along with the Gulf monarchs. Until then, the monarchs' conservative traditionalism would naturally attract the support of these groups. Only the New Middle Class, an emerging group of liberal technocrats with a penchant for representative government, could, most writers agreed, pose a threat to these monarchs, and that small threat could be forestalled with a judicious application of money and force. Even writers working from a dependency perspective arrive at more or less the same conclusion.

The rentier state literature, like its predecessors, also presents, albeit in a very different way, a view of civil society as fundamentally weak. Several writers (myself included) have argued that oil revenues empower the state at the expense of society. Oil revenues allow the state to undercut existing social groups and to preempt the formation of new ones. These revenues allow the state to lavishly provide resources—from jobs to housing to welfare—that other social groups once provided or would have come to provide in the absence of such wealthy states. Revenues also give the state the power to weaken social groups by co-opting them collectively or by fragmenting them through selective co-optation of key members. Oil revenues allow the state to weaken civil society.

Although this image of the Gulf is in some ways accurate, it is incomplete. The rentier literature helps us understand why societal pressures for change might be muted and why governments might be more able to contain even these muted pressures. It is certainly true that the Gulf monarchs have shown a considerable antipathy to organized groups, even groups with the most apparently apolitical intentions. They have gone to some lengths to prevent, preempt, or destroy a variety of social organizations. Nonetheless, despite their best efforts, incipient pressures from Islamist, human rights, tribal, technocratic, and other groups have in fact appeared in the Gulf. Important, organized, and independent groups with interests that demand to be accommodated are alive in the Gulf, actively petitioning the rulers. A variety of important groups has, in fact, emerged, survived, or transformed since independence, and since oil. In order to comprehend the impulses behind civil society, and the utility of the concept itself, it is necessary to understand both the nature of social stratification—the array of groups, the kinds of interests that persistently cluster—and the mechanisms that connect these strata to each other and to those in power.

15

Civil Society Against the War System: The Lebanese Case

Antoine Messarra

Civil war infected Lebanon for fifteen years, from 1975–1990. During this period a system of militia organizations and parties dominated the country, including the media and the economy. Indeed, the militias extracted massive sums from the Lebanese economy. For instance, billions of dollars were siphoned from the Beirut port, where militias displaced the state and collected customs duties. In all, the militias seized about fifteen billion dollars, or one billion dollars per year from the port. This does not include import and export taxes collected throughout the country by the militias, or profits earned in the drug trade, which also totaled about one billion dollars per year, or the value of weapons seized from the Lebanese army, totaling another one billion dollars. Thus, the war system that emerged in Lebanon controlled massive financial resources. The militia parties consolidated their control in sectarian zones or cantons. Those opposing the war system were sometimes assassinated, and intimidation of political personalities as well as the press was common. Nonetheless, civil society in Lebanon, which opposed the war system, not only survived but proved to be remarkably assertive in expressing opposition to the war system.

Among those segments of civil society that actively opposed the war system were the National Union of Lebanese Workers, the Lawyers Union, and the National Union of Teachers. For instance, in October 1987, to protest the deteriorating political and economic conditions in the country, Lebanese teachers representing all major confessional groups launched a national strike. For its part, the lawyers union refused to hold elections so long as parts of the membership were prevented from participating. Over the course of the late 1980s, several important demonstrations, bringing together diverse Lebanese, were held to protest the continuing civil war. The largest was organized by the National Union of Workers and involved about three hundred thousand participants or 10 percent of Lebanon's population.

The Lebanese case illustrates the durability of Lebanon's civil society, although much remains to be done to consolidate and protect basic human rights and freedom since the civil war ended in 1990. Having considered this case, it is appropriate to inquire about the requisites for fostering civil society in the Arab world in general. These requisites include:

• Laws to protect the rights of citizens, including the right to establish associations, the rights of women, and laws that preserve the autonomy of Arab universities and protect them from state control.
• The instilling of the values of citizenship, including tolerance, democracy and the respect for individual liberties.

From "al-mujtama' al-madani fi mujabahah nidham al-harb: al-halah al-lub-naniyyah," an unpublished paper presented in Giza, Egypt, May 1992

16

Palestinian Civil Society

Muhammad Muslih

When the Oslo Agreement was signed in Washington, D.C., on 13 September 1993, many Palestinians were angered by the numerous concessions unilaterally accepted by PLO (Palestine Liberation Organization) Chairman Yasir Arafat, and the fact that the agreement emerged from secret negotiations between Israel and the PLO, rather than through the ongoing bilateral talks initiated in Madrid in 1991. The debate raises important questions concerning the extent to which Palestinian civil society should play a direct role in creating and legitimizing an entity or state. Judging from the ability of Palestinian associational life to endure internal as well as external pressures, it is not difficult to imagine that the infrastructure of political and civic institutions that would support a Palestinian state—whenever that state arrives—may well emerge from the diverse formations of Palestinian civil society.

Although associational life among Palestinians living in the West Bank and Gaza has long been rich, critics have questioned whether the concept of civil society can be applied to their various associational forms. In this regard, two unique aspects of the Palestinian situation pose difficulties for studying civil society in relation to the state. First, the Palestinians have not had a national government in the twentieth century. Since 1967, the Israeli occupation apparatus has functioned as the de facto authority in the West Bank and Gaza. The Palestinians consider the Israeli military regime illegitimate, and their goal is not simply to undermine its control or to temper its arbitrary effects but to dismantle it altogether.

Second, prior to the signing of the Israeli-PLO Declaration of Principles (also known as the Oslo Agreement), Palestinians in the occupied territories accepted an external actor, the PLO, as their "state," clandestinely cooperating with local PLO representatives to sustain a network of institutions through which the PLO sought to exercise political power in competition with the Israeli military regime. With the signing of the declaration and the exchange of PLO and Israeli letters of mutual recognition on 9 September

1993, the PLO has become an internal actor that aspires to replace the authority of the Israeli occupier in the West Bank and Gaza. The behavior of the PLO toward its constituency in the occupied territories will have an impact on the organs of civil society in these territories.

The characteristics of society in the occupied territories also influence Palestinian associational life. The essence of social organization is a network of *hamulat* (extended families) and smaller families as well as village, neighborhood, and religious solidarities. Palestinian society is mainly rural in character, and even urban centers are closer to the model of a small town than to that of a metropolitan area. Even in Gaza, where close to 85 percent of the inhabitants reside in the town itself, the culture is predominantly rural.

This raises interesting questions germane to the study of civil society in a Palestinian context. Can a society with dominant rural characteristics, essentially organized on the basis of lineage, produce enduring civil society organs that transcend local solidarities? Should Palestinian civil society be studied in the context of statelessness? These questions may be addressed within the framework of the "state surrogate" paradigm. The concept of "state surrogate," as used here, is political rather than sociological and refers to the PLO. As a para-state formation, the PLO has many of the underpinnings of a government, including a bureaucracy, an army, financial resources, and, in the West Bank and Gaza, a network of institutions through which it tries to exercise political power. Placing civil society organs in this perspective will help to throw light on the prospects for democratization during the five-year transitional period of Palestinian interim self-government authority and beyond.

17

Civil Society in the Gaza Strip

Sara Roy

The problem of civil society in the Arab world has emerged as a central issue in contemporary Arab intellectual discourse, catalyzed as much by the crisis and collapse of the Soviet and Eastern European states as by the strength of their popular, oppositional civil social movements. The absence or weakness of Arab civil society is now seen as one cause of the contemporary crisis in Arab politics and its contributing factors: the absence of democracy, the lack of political change and participation, continued economic underdevelopment and social malaise, and the persistence of human rights violations.

Although the concept of civil society does carry arguable explanatory weight, its significance for Arab society lies fundamentally in why it is so intensely debated: It represents an attempt on the part of the Arab citizen to deal with the issues of political repression and personal oppression. Perhaps nowhere, at present, is this attempt more pronounced than in the Gaza Strip. This is so because of the very unprecedented political, economic, and social possibilities created by the Israeli-PLO agreement on interim self-government arrangements.

One of the greatest problems facing civil society in Gaza is recreating and maintaining solidarity among disparate social actors. The beginning of limited self-rule and the establishment of a Palestinian national authority in the Gaza Strip and Jericho are seen by many as the first and necessary step toward Gaza's social reconstruction. Perhaps it is. However, the legal context of self-rule and the behavior of the Palestinian National Authority (PNA) suggest otherwise. The former, as defined by the terms of the agreement signed in Cairo on 4 May 1994, is designed to retain the status quo of occupation. For example, according to these terms, Israeli military law will remain in effect during the interim period and the autonomous areas will remain under the control of the occupation regime. Furthermore, the Palestinian authority has no real power to change the law since Israel retains a veto over all Palestinian legislation. Hence, the occupation continues; only its form has changed, and the PNA is there, in effect, to manage it. Under such conditions, what form should resistance assume?

Arafat is playing on the very pronounced divisions and tensions that now exist between Gaza's refugee and indigenous communities. After decades of disparity and discrimination, the refugees feel that they are entitled to greater reward than their indigenous counterparts who are seen not to have suffered as deeply or as consistently. This is one of the most ominous social divisions emerging in Gaza. Unlike the West Bank, where there is a strong middle class and many established wealthy families from which to draw political support, in Gaza, there is the predominant refugee population, Gaza's largest social class. As such, they constitute an important source of support and a perceived political lever against future competitors, particularly the Islamists. Arafat has made his bias clear by appointing refugees to a number of important political positions.

Is there any reason to believe that a Palestinian government will make itself more accessible to the sometime involvement of the people, as a legitimate state authority is expected to do in its relations with civil society? Perhaps more important, within the structure and terms of the autonomy agreement, how much freedom does the PNA actually have to do what is needed to build a genuine Palestinian civil society, assuming of course that it is trying to do so?

For their part, Gazans must confront and address other challenges if they are to make their society more civil. They must acknowledge their own dependency on the outside world and their self-indulgent image of themselves as victim. They must confront their own cycle of violence and oppression, their lack of law-abidingness, their conflict between secular and religious identity, and the erosion of their national identity. They must deal with the fact that authoritarian and oppressive disciplines continue to be practiced within the family, the community, and institutions, including political institutions. They must address an intellectual life that is weak and a cultural life that is poor. They must confront the continued oppression of their women. Indeed, if the highly prized pluralism of civil society exists in Gaza, it is the plurality of oppressions.

Gazans greatly fear the imposition of another repressive regime—this time Palestinian. Many increasingly see a connection between emerging Palestinian authoritarianism and Israel's security-led interpretation of autonomy. Gazans say they will resist. But how? What mechanisms of social and political mediation, other than violence, do Gazans really have at their disposal? Put differently, what does it mean to be an autonomous, socially engaged person in Gaza today, in an environment characterized by continuing occupation, waning security, warring factions, a moribund economy, diminishing water and land, a traumatized population, and an uneducated generation of children? Tragically for Gaza, the possibility of civil unrest appears greater than the capacity of civil society to address it.

18

Early Elections in the West Bank and Gaza

Jillian Schwedler

There is a surprising lack of debate on the potential for early elections among the Palestinians in the West Bank and Gaza to propel the Israeli-Palestinian dialogue over outstanding issues. Viewing elections only as an outcome of a peaceful, negotiated settlement ignores the potential for early elections to serve as an impetus rather than a result.

What are the obstacles to holding such elections? Many Palestinians insist that Palestinians who were living in the West Bank and Gaza in 1967 must have the right to vote in the event national elections are held, even if they have lived outside the territories since the 1967 war. The Israeli government continues to reject these terms, as allowing the participation of Palestinians outside the occupied territories would signal acceptance of Palestinian right-of-return arguments, something even Labor leadership is not prepared to do.

Clearly, one cannot realistically envision large-scale elections until a tangible solution to the region's myriad conflicts are resolved. As an alternative, early elections may provide momentum to the peace process. Palestinian participation in peaceful, fair elections would demonstrate to Israel and the international community a commitment to the peaceful resolution of regional conflicts. Gradually, legitimate Palestinian political institutions would emerge throughout the occupied territories, allowing Israeli officials to become more comfortable with expanded Palestinian autonomy.

The very timing of elections may be the catalyst in the diplomatic process. As an independent variable, early elections may provide the framework for a spirit of trust and cooperation to develop. At this juncture, elections among the Palestinians in the West Bank and Gaza to select a new, legitimate Palestinian authority could lend decisive impetus to the rapid settlement of outstanding issues.

In addition to rethinking the timing of elections, other variables should be reexamined. Elections of limited scope, at local rather than national levels, could also be held outside the context of outstanding issues. Municipal and associational elections, for example, provide civilian sectors with a mechanism for addressing their grievances. Indeed, elections within Palestinian civil society have been held for years, and occasional local municipal elections have achieved moderate success. Palestinian civil society is vibrant and strong; allowing a Palestinian political superstructure to take shape gradually would assure Israel that any autonomy granted to the Palestinians of the West Bank and Gaza is established in the spirit of democracy and civility.

  The assumption that elections will only follow a comprehensive political settlement obscures the potential for early elections to build confidence. Through the fostering of a climate of cooperation and peaceful coexistence, even the most reluctant would benefit.

From "Early Elections in the West Bank and Gaza," *Middle East Insight,* July–October 1993

19

The Destruction of
Civil Society in the Sudan

Ann Mosely Lesch

Civil society is a multifaceted concept, comprising the idea of autonomous associations, the concept of civility, and the role of government as rule setter and facilitator. Autonomous associations provide a buffer between the individual and the power of the state. Civility implies tolerance: respect for different viewpoints and social attitudes, accepting the idea that there is no single right answer, and sharing a sense of citizenship. The government role is also essential as rule setter, referee, and protector of civil society, since it establishes criteria for citizenship and sets the legal rules under which associations operate.

In Sudan, associational life is severely restricted and is prevented by the government from serving as a buffer between the individual and the state. Autonomous trade and professional unions, student councils, and economic structures are systematically suppressed. Independent political parties and newspapers are banned. Christian and Muslim religious organizations are closely monitored, curtailed, and sometimes closed. No public dissent is tolerated by the regime.

Instead, Islamist associations monopolize the political, economic, and social arenas. National Islamic Front (NIF) adherents dominate the civil service, schools, and diplomatic service. They control the security and military apparatuses, operate parallel intelligence, police, and paramilitary forces, and virtually monopolize major economic sectors, including international trade, oil, agriculture, and industry. The Islamist totalizing agenda seeks to transform the personality as well as the behavior of the Sudanese citizens. They enforce a rigorous version of the Islamic penal code, restrict the behavior of women, compel non-Muslims and non-Arabs to study Islamic beliefs and use Arabic, and force adult males to undergo "reeducation" programs. The Islamists aim to create a homogeneous national identity, through fostering Islamist norms and suppressing alternative values and views. Differences are viewed as illegitimate and divisive.

Those policies have destroyed the civil society that was emerging in the Sudan from 1985 to 1989. During those four years, a wide range of autonomous political, economic, social, and religious organizations expressed diverse views and perspectives. Despite a tendency toward anarchy, given the proliferation of groups and the ongoing unresolved debate on the national identity of the Sudan, the country moved toward creating a sense of citizenship and establishing increasingly clear rules of fair play. Even the legitimacy of the territorial boundaries of the country was enhanced, as the diverse groups contested for power in the center rather than calling for secession. Nonetheless, acceptance of a definition of citizenship that incorporated differences remained incomplete, and thus, the country was still vulnerable to the actions of a minority that rejected that definition.

The totalizing policies of the NIF regime have not only undermined those efforts to create a civil society but have also reopened core questions of national identity. The drive to silence opponents and suppress alternative beliefs has resulted in renewed calls for secession by the south. Since non-Islamist identities are denied, a separate geographic state has become increasingly desirable to many citizens. Dissidents have had to grapple with the difficulty of articulating a Sudanese identity that will respect the differences among its peoples. Even though some Sudanese politicians and intellectuals have attempted to create in exile alternative institutions that are based on democratic norms, they remain divided on basic issues involving ethnicity and the role of religion in society.

Renewing the effort to establish a civil society remains problematic. Even if the regime is overthrown, it will be difficult to undo the structural changes, recreate the autonomous institutions, and reestablish trust among the diverse social forces.

20

State, Civil Society, and Political Change in Syria

Raymond A. Hinnebusch

In Syria, authoritarian rule appears remarkably durable in spite of the increasing socioeconomic modernization that arguably broadens the base of pluralism. Is Syria a true case of "Middle Eastern exceptionalism"? The connection between social differentiation and political pluralization in Syria has been diluted by many intervening variables that raise the pluralist threshold. One such variable is the fragility of civil society.

Syria's historic experience shows that pluralism is retarded in the absence of a balance whereby an institutionalized state incorporates an autonomous civil society. The premodern imperial state tolerated civil society, but it was fragmented and malintegrated into the political structure. The burst of new association generated by postindependence modernization broadened civil society, but political mobilization amidst sharp class cleavages could not be contained by a fragile liberal polity unrooted in an indigenous state tradition.

The authority vacuum was filled by the rise of an authoritarian state. The Ba'th revolution created a more open social structure and a more class-inclusive form of authoritarian-corporatist polity. But this stronger state also deadened the fragile political life of the pluralist era. A large public sector clientelized society, and international conflict fueled a huge national security apparatus.

The overdeveloped state deprived much of civil society of its autonomy but never wholly suffocated it; indeed, its rudiments or bases persisted or even widened under the Ba'th. First, the traditional city remained resistant to state penetration, an alternative society with many aspects of civility, a partially autonomous economic base, and a counterideology. The artisanal and merchant petite bourgeoisie, far from declining under the Ba'th, flourished in the vacuum left by the demise of the haute bourgeoisie and in spaces left by gaps in state control. Second, the Ba'th state's development drive, in fostering a proliferation of social forces enjoying more diversified resources, broadened the formerly circumscribed bases of civil society. Increases in educational opportunity, urbanization, and modern occupations socially mobilized Syria on a major scale and generated a large salaried middle class. As professionals and skilled workers proliferated, so did membership in syndicates, ostensible networks of civil society that could take on autonomous life, were government controls to be relaxed. Third, an independent bourgeoisie, the force most able to carve out some room for civil society by checking state power, is reviving. By the late 1970s, as the political elite underwent embourgeoisement, the state began to foster the reconstruction of a bourgeoisie, with state-linked and private wings. When rent-driven economic growth declined in the 1980s the state began to shed some of its economic responsibilities. Private business had to be given concessions to fill the economic gap and by the 1990s the regime regarded it not just as an auxiliary to the public sector but as a second engine of growth. The private sector's share of foreign trade and investment widened rapidly and new private industries proliferated. The bourgeoisie is still too state-dependent, fragmented, and weak to confront the state, but it may be widening the space for civil society.

This will not produce democratization any time soon. The regime deploys such still-viable substitutes for pluralism as clientalism and corporatism while holding repression in reserve. But Syria is undergoing a limited liberalization as the regime adapts its rule to the exhaustion of "statist" development. The president is broadening his base beyond the party, and groups have won more freedom to advocate their interests. Government controls over society are being incrementally relaxed, possibly allowing a more autonomous civil society to emerge as a base for future political pluralization.

From *Civil Society in the Middle East,* vol. 2

21

Civil Society in Formation: Tunisia

Eva Bellin

Among the countries of the Arab world, Tunisia is uniquely well-positioned to expand the boundaries of civil society and beat back the domain of despotism. First, Tunisian citizens share that overarching sense of political community so essential to the development of a "civic culture" but so rare in the Arab world. Tunisian society is relatively unfragmented by ethnic or religious cleavage (more than 98 percent of Tunisians are Sunni Muslims and the Arab/Berber cleavage has diminished to near political insignificance over the past hundred years). Moreover, the country has enjoyed a protracted experience of political identity long predating the era of colonial mapmaking. Second, the country has had a long history of civilian rule during which past president Bourguiba purposely contracted the size of the military and subordinated it firmly to civilian control. There is no powerful military competing with (or doubling as) the ruling party in Tunisia as is the case in many other countries in the region. Third, the state's long-held policy to promote education and widely spread the benefits of economic development has endowed the country with a large and relatively well-educated middle class. This generates precisely the sort of citizens who might possess the skills and leisure necessary to develop *civisme* and use democratic institutions effectively. Fourth, Tunisia was among the first Arab countries to break with "Arab socialism" and embark on a "quasi-liberal" strategy of development (at least in the sense of consciously promoting the development of private sector commerce and industry). Hence the state created space for the development of autonomous sources of economic power that might imaginably countervail it one day. Fifth, and perhaps most important, the state has publicly committed itself to the development of civil society in Tunisia. Thus, even if public policy has not always kept pace with official discourse, the state's public prizing of a Montesquieuian model of polity provides a legitimating ideological wedge for citizens lobbying on its behalf.

Still, there is no reason to be complacent about the development of civil society in Tunisia. Although the country has made notable progress in combating some common sources of despotism (nurturing a culture of *civisme* and civility, dispersing the loci of economic power in society, expanding the reach of some democratic institutions), it has still failed to achieve one important goal—the institutionalization of contestation sufficient to impose accountability upon a despotically tempted state. The responsibility for this failure lies squarely with the state, driven as it is by contradictory impulses to foster civil society but contain its development so as not to cede political control. These contradictory impulses are evident in the state's management of associational life, economic liberalization, and the extension of civil liberties, three important trajectories in the development of civil society in Tunisia. Tunisia's experience in each of these areas illustrates the state's contradictory agenda and its role in shaping the strengths and weaknesses of civil society in Tunisia today.

From *Civil Society in the Middle East,* vol. 1

22

Notes on Civil Society in Tunisia

Abdelbaki Hermassi

The historical formation of civil society in Tunisia is best viewed in terms of an accumulation of consecutive layers, from the traditional associations through the colonialist and nationalist periods, to the corporatist associations and current diversification.

Traditional associations are the very old associations, such as groups that managed water distribution, *awqaf* (charitable foundations), and philanthropic associations designed to assist students and provide health care and other services to the poor. Others serve to finance marriages, cover funeral services, and lessen the risk of certain commercial activities. Islamic brotherhoods and Sufi orders also served these functions, although the services were provided only to members.

The next layer of associational life emerged during the colonial encounter. In the late nineteenth century, the need to create a modern elite led the French to create *al-Khalduniyyah,* a "society" of civil character with a cultural orientation. As a club and forum, its teaching and activities sought to link modernity and *asalah* (rootedness). In 1923, the first labor union called for the formation of cooperatives to help organize traders and artisans hit by the competition and economic crisis. With the National Front in power in 1936, legislation in the social realm favored associational life in almost every respect. Unions, political parties, professional associations, and art academies were all encouraged. Even sports clubs and women's associations emerged. Together, these groups allowed Tunisian civil society to express itself through new avenues outside of the direct political or syndical channels.

The *Destour* Party gradually established control over these organizations and created new ones in sectors where the party thought a supporting constituency would be crucial. It created and supported congenial organizations in almost every significant sector of society: workers, peasants, businessmen, students, women, and youth. Because many of these groups were not very involved during national mobilizations for independence, they managed to retain a margin of autonomy.

With independence, however, these groups fell under direct state control. One sector after another came to be covered by one single association that cared more about being in line with the state party than about the constituency it was supposed to represent. The typical corporatist association is created by statute and endowed with a formal monopoly of representation for all who work in the field of jurisdiction. Membership is generally compulsory, providing the organization with a guaranteed income that is supplemented by government subsidies. By the 1960s and 1970s, this corporatist system of interest representation was operating smoothly.

For most of the past thirty years, primacy was given to the state over civil society. Initiatives came from the state, while civil society was taught, educated, "improved," and, of course, watched and controlled. However, although the corporatist structure may have been efficient during the "socialist" decade of the 1960s and the economic *infitah* (liberalization) of the 1970s, the strategy has proven costly. The absence of a free space for social and political expression forced dissenting voices (including Islamists and university students) into substitute political arenas. This emergence of opposition movements and rise of mass movements in cities led the government to reevaluate its traditional hostility toward civil society. Tunisian society had grown more differentiated, and thirty years of independence had broadened the people's vision of what they could and should be able to do. But in order to accommodate pluralism while preventing the emergence of autonomous centers of power, the government has begun to allow more struggle for representation while rejecting the repression of diversity. As a result, the prospects for civil society in Tunisia will depend on whether the government maintains this strategy.

From an unpublished paper presented in Giza, Egypt, May 1992

23

Civil Society in Turkey

Binnaz Toprak

The development of civil society is contingent upon the existence of a state tradition. Whereas a strong state may hamper the individual's autonomy from it, thus constraining associational activity that is free from state control, a civil society without the state's enforcement of universal legal norms and guarantee of civil rights is equally a danger to individual freedom. In Muslim contexts, this requires the separation of religion from the state, given the unequal treatment in Islamic law of women, non-Muslims, and nonbelievers. Hence, a conception of the public sphere that does not define public roles in terms of religious affiliation, ethnicity, kinship, or gender is an important prerequisite of civil society. This is the dividing line between civil society as free space, reflecting individual choice and peaceful collective action that recognize the right of other social actors to pursue equally valid claims for individual expression and choice of public policy, versus civil society that functions under public law that recognizes the cogency of particularistic criteria. Once the state gives up its claim to enforce universal legal norms, the individual is left defenseless against communal definitions of morality, gender roles, racial prejudice, and so forth. In such settings, a vibrant civil society may exist with its plethora of organizations, while, at the same time, certain groups are excluded from exerting influence, or even unhampered appearance, in the public sphere. The status of women living under states that follow Islamic law and the previous status of blacks in the United States are notable examples.

This understanding of civil society inspires the discussion of the Turkish case. Although a strong state tradition in Turkey often constricted the formation of a free space for organized social action, it allowed, at the same time, for political opposition to formulate alternative public policy in terms of the very principle that the Turkish state had accepted, namely, equality before the law. Thus, civil society in Turkey must be understood in terms of the tensions created by the bureaucratic structure and the official ideology of the Republic, on the one hand, and increased demands for recognition by minority groups, on the other. In this context, the feminist agenda, the Islamist movement, and Kurdish separatism are all critical issues for the discussion of a vibrant public sphere.

The political and economic changes following the 1980 coup drew considerable attention to the concept of civil society among various groups who identified the problems of democracy in Turkey in terms of state-society relations. Thus, issues such as the consolidation of democracy, civil rights, civilian-military relations, and organizational activity can be fruitfully discussed with references to recent examples in the field of legislation and responses from civil society.

24

Authoritarian Secularism and Islamic Participation: The Case of Turkey

Nilüfer Göle

In the Middle East, inherent tensions exist between the implementation of secularism and the transition to democracy, on the one hand, and authoritarian modernism and Islamic participation, on the other. Secularism, in other words, does not appear as a neutral, power-free principle: It underlines the political and cultural power of the Western elite. Throughout the region, however, the reassertion of Islam in politics has been one of the ideological tools for the empowerment of civil society.

Contemporary Islamic radicalism manifests a challenge to an authoritarian mode of modernism and the equation established between the "civilized" and the "Westernized." It promotes the return of Muslim actors on the historical scene, along with their own ethics and esthetics. Yet, such a "return of the repressed" not only takes the form of the rejection of the West and the "revenge of popular masses" but also the form of Islamic elite who reappropriate some of the acquisitions of modernity, primarily concerning education, and participate in the production of values and the symbolic cultural capital.

In the national cases where there is a possibility for the circulation (alternation) of elites through the education system, upward social mobility, and democratic elections, Islamist movements tend to be more participatory in their logic of action. Turkey might provide such an example. Conversely, in countries where channels of upward social mobility and political participation are repressed, the social ascension of the Islamist elites is blocked and the Islamist movement will likely evolve toward a logic of reaction and/or violence. The closeness of the ties between the popular masses and the elites is also very illustrative of the nature of the Islamic movement. Islamic movements can move in the directions of participatory and interactive politics to the extent that they succeed in establishing and acknowledging their own elites.

Therefore, it is social practice, rather than some sort of essence of Islam, that will determine the totalizing or democratic nature of Islamic movements. The compatibility of democracy and Islamist movements depends upon the self-limitation of the totalizing Islamist project and the enhancement of pluralism in general. The interaction and the establishment of horizontal relations between different social actors and political ideologies are basic prerequisites of political pluralism and the autonomy of civil society. Only the building up of a consensual politics at the level of civil society can countercheck the totalitarian tendencies embedded in utopian oppositional movements and raise the chances for democratic participation.

25

Yemen Between
Civility and Civil War

Sheila Carapico

Many scholars and interested observers, Westerners and Arabs alike, argue that Arab culture has not produced a "civil society" that could provide a basis for democratic practice. If these arguments apply to the Arab world generally, they would seem to doubly characterize Yemen, the quintessential traditional Arab society, deeply imbued with Islamic values, tenaciously attached to tribal and regional loyalties, armed to the teeth, and absent any history of liberal or pluralist government. These arguments may be evaluated in light of the Yemeni experience between unification in May 1990, and the outbreak of war almost exactly four years later.

Several themes are noteworthy. First, Yemeni organizations tended to be backward even by Egyptian, Jordanian, or North African standards, straddling the line between tribal or primordial and civic affiliation and practice. Secondly, there was the peculiar brand of Yemeni "corporatism," a kind of "bait and switch" strategy whereby for every independent civil society action—a conference, or the formation of a new NGO (nongovernment organization)—a comparable but competing effort was launched by the government. So, for virtually every NGO, there was a GO-NGO (government-organized NGO). Thirdly, despite these circumstances, and, indeed, despite Yemen's neighbors' opposition to its democratic experiment, its president's preference for rule-by-decree, the crude presence of military checkpoints along urban and intercity thoroughfares, and the nearly constant threat of redivision of the country, Yemen did get a taste of political pluralism. Conferences, political campaigns, newspaper debates, and welfare associations helped diffuse and/or channel the mass frustrations over inflation, corruption, and unfairness.

It is true that Yemen took no more than a tentative step along the road to constitutional, representative, responsive government, and the experiment ended when both former ruling parties tired of debate and one of them chased the other into exile. Moreover, if civil society consists of letterheads, bylaws, and Robert's Rules of Order, then it was nowhere to be found. Surely Yemen bore little semblance to the ideal-typical democracy some Yemenis presume exists in the West—or even, for that matter, to the dense NGO environment in Egypt.

Still, the evidence illuminates a civil-society-in-the-making, a clearing of the political space between primordial affiliations and the central state to make room for pluralist debate, a tug-of-war between regimes inaugurated by force of arms and popular demands for the rule of law, a situation where the security apparatus was temporarily restrained in its use of intimidation, where instead of being jailed journalists were brought to court, and where former ruling parties went to extraordinary lengths to secure electoral victory for their candidates and a parliamentary majority for their proposals. Tribal and national conferences applied pressure on the regime to hold elections, and the national and Ta'iz conferences put forth a Code of Political Conduct, a modified version of which both ruling parties were obliged to endorse. Along with the December 1992 street demonstrations, the press, seminars, and NGO activities helped impel the system toward fulfillment of the promise for elections. In the postelection period, discussions and exposés applied further pressure to postpone discussion of the constitutional amendments and then to mediate the government crisis of late 1993 and early 1994. Massive participation by thousands of the country's leading figures in meetings, conferences, and discussions in December, January, and February attempted to prevent war from breaking out. The fact that this movement failed cannot be taken as evidence that it never existed at all.

Conclusion: Civil Society and Political Reform in the Middle East

Farhad Kazemi
Augustus Richard Norton

Looking at contested politics in the Middle East and the strategies available for political reform to the regimes in power, regimes have three ideal-typical strategies in dealing with political pressures from within—inclusion, exclusion, or repression. A policy of inclusion assumes a basic understanding, acceptance, and appreciation of the rules of the game by both the regime and its adversaries. It accepts the notion that power and governance may be shared in principle as well as the possibility that one's adversary may in fact gain ultimate political power. It further assumes that the rules of the game will not be changed unilaterally by a single contestant that happens to be at the helm of power.

In contrast, a policy of exclusion rejects the notion that power may be shared by the adversaries even if the rules of the game are observed. Adversaries' roles and actions are considered serious threats to the survival of the regime and the state. Opponents can "play ball" only if they accept the regime as the ultimate arbiter and the paramount decisionmaker in the political arena. In other words, it is either acceptance or exclusion.

A variant of a policy of exclusion is the attempt to keep opponents from power-sharing through calculated, purposeful, and organized collective force by the state. In such a situation the regime in power uses its monopoly of means of physical violence to prevent the emergence of the adversaries as claimants to power. Alternately, it will use the arm of the state to crush opponents who have managed to emerge through illicit and underground means.

Given the fundamental economic, social, and political problems in the Middle East, strategies of exclusion and repression will be increasingly difficult to sustain over the long run. The fact that many Middle Eastern regimes suffer from eroded political legitimacy, and the resultant insecurity of the rulers, implies that only a gradual program of reform is likely to be palatable to the present governments (and their supporters).

What exacerbates contested politics in the Middle East is the role of the Islamist militant political organizations as the main adversaries of many of the regimes. Although the Islamist groups are by no means monolithic, the underlying fear of them as groups determined to impose a rigid Islamic code, their version of the Islamic law *(shari'ah),* on the social order has created major additional obstacles to possibilities of power-sharing. Some regimes contend that the Islamists' concept of citizenship and rules of governance are profoundly religious and exclusionary. Thus, their acceptance of the rules of the game is instrumentalist—designed for political gain when they lack control over the institutions of the state. This will change, the argument goes, when they come to power and decide to impose their restrictive norms on the polity. Once in power, they will not allow opponents any political voice and will reject categorically all attempts at power-sharing by non-Islamists.

Although this argument may be valid and relevant to some groups in the Middle East, it cannot be used across the board as the justification for refusal to share power through the ballot box. In fact, there are significant differences among the Islamist groups on many basic issues, and it would be a mistake to lump them together as one unitary group with a unidimensional and divinely inspired vision of politics. Furthermore, not all contestants for political power are Islamist in orientation. There are others in the social system whose demands for political reform and liberalization do not stem necessarily from the religious perspective. They cannot, therefore, be rejected on the grounds of adherence to a rigid system of religious orthodoxy.

One can elucidate the parameters of contested politics by analyzing the state-society interactions in the Middle East, in part by reviewing and analyzing the relevant pressures and forces in the social system and civil society that have laid the foundations for contested politics and burgeoning political demands.

The following schematic presents the argument that frames the book:

(1) Middle Eastern governments are often marked by ineffectualness and declining legitimacy, and the already awesome burdens that they confront are growing. (2) Access to a variety of "rents" has allowed many governments to lower the stakes of politics and buy off dissent. (3) The end of the Cold War, major progress toward the resolution of the Arab-Israeli conflict, and weak oil prices have reduced rents and therefore decreased the resources available to government. (4) Although economic and political reform seems imperative, the authoritarian state remains in control and is reluctant to cede power or even open up government. (5) Even when political reformers emerge, they must confront the legacy of authoritarianism: stunted civil societies. (6) Indeed, government policies have tended to priv-

ilege populist Islamist forces, sometimes by design, but often as a side effect of the suppression of potential opponents among the secular opposition. (7) Governments must choose between strategies of reform and inclusion, on the one hand, or strategies of exclusion and repression, on the other. (8) The study argues that the imperative of reform is overdetermined, and that strategies of exclusion and campaigns of repression are losing games in the long run. (9) Barring unlikely economic windfall, most Middle Eastern governments will have little choice but to pursue incremental but purposeful reform.

From *Civil Society in the Middle East*

Bibliography

Arabic-Language Sources

'Abd al-Basit 'Abd al-Mu'ti and Ibrahim Hasan al-Issawi, *Dirasat al-takwin al-ijtima'i wa al-tabaqi li misr: al-dirasat al-mahalliyyah* (Cairo: National Center for Sociological and Criminological Research, 1988, 1989).

'Abd al-Hadi, Izzat, *Al-intifadah wa ba'd qadaya al-tanmiyyah al-sha'biyyah* (Ramallah: Bisan Press, 1992).

'Abd al-Mun'im, Ahmad Faris, "Jama'at al-masalih wa al-sulta al-siyasiyyah fi misr: dirasat 'ala al-niqabat al-mihaniyyah, al-muhamin, wa al-sahafiyyin wa al-muhandisin fi al-fatrah, 1952–1961," Ph.D. dissertation, Cairo University, 1984.

Abid al-Jabiri, Muhammad, "Ishkaliyyah al-dimuqratiyyah wa al-mujtama' al-madini fi al-watan al-'arabi," *al-Mustaqbil al-'Arabi* 167, no. 1 (January 1993).

Abu Amr, Ziad, *Al-harakah al-islamiyyah fi al-diffah al-gharbiyyah wa qita' ghazzah* (Akka: Dar al-Aswar, 1989).

Abu Amshah, Adil, *Al-awda' al-iqtisadiyyah wa al-ijtima'iyyah fi al-diffah al-gharbiyyah wa qita' ghazzah qabla wa athna' al-intifadah* (Nablus: al-Najah University, 1989).

Ahmad, Rif'at Sayyid, *Al-nabi al-musallah: al-rafidun,* second document (London: Riad al-Rayyis Books Ltd., 1991).

———, *Al-nabi al-musallah: al-tha'irun* (London: Riad al-Rayyid Books Ltd., 1991).

'Amarah, Muhammad, *Al-kilafah wa nash'at al-ahzab al-siyasiyyah* (Beirut: Al-Mu'assasah al-'Arabiyyah li al-Dirasat al-Nashr, 1977).

Amr Bsalm, Hussayn, *Dallil al-sihafah al-yamaniyyah* (Sana'a, Mu'assassah al-Thawrah al-Sihafah, 1992).

'Ata, 'Abd al-Khabir Mahmud, "Al-harakah al-islamiyyah wa qadiyat al-ta'addudiyyah," *Al-majallat al-'arabiyyah li al-'ulum al-siyasiyyah, nos. 5 and 6, (April 1992), pp. 115–116.

'Awa, Muhammad S., "Al-ta'addudiyyah min manzur islami," *Minbar al-Hiwar* 6, no. 20 (Winter 1991): 134–136.

Barakat, Muhammad T., *Sayyid Qutb: khulasat hayatuh, minhajuhuh fi al-harakah wa al-naqd al-muwajah ilayh* (Beirut: Dar al-Da'wah, 1970s).

Barghouty, Iyad, *Al-aslamah wa al-siyasah fi al-aradi al-filastiniyyah al-muhtallah* (Jerusalem: Al-Zahra' Center, 1990).

———, "Al-Islam bayna al-sultah wa al-mu'aradah," *Qadayah fikriyyah: Al-islam al-siyasi, al-usus al-fikriyyah wa al-ahdaf al-'amalliyyah* (Cairo: Dar al-Thaqafah al-Jadidah, 1989).

Bedaoui, Abdeljelil, et al., "Al-mu'assassat al-niqabiyyah al-'ummaliyyah fi tunis: hususatiah, dawriah, 'uzmatiah," *Utruhat* 10 (1986).

89

Boutros, Huwayda A. R., "Al-dawr al-siyasi li al-harakah al-'ummaliyyah fi misr, 1952–1982," M.A. thesis, Cairo University, 1990.

al-Bushri, Tariq, "'An mu'assassat al-dawlah fi al-nuzum al-islamiyyah wa al-'arabiyyah," *Minbar al-Hiwar,* no. 19 (Summer 1989), pp. 74–79, 89.

Center for Arab Unity Studies, *Al-mujtama' al-madani fi al-watan al-'arabi* (Beirut: CAUS, 1992).

Center for Political and Strategic Studies, *Intikhabat majlis al-sha'b: dirasah wa tahlil* (Cairo: CPSS, 1986, 1988, 1992).

———, *Al-taqrir al-istratiji al-'arabi, 1990* (Cairo: Dar al-Ahram, 1991).

———, *Al-taqrir al-istratiji al-'arabi, 1989* (Cairo: Dar al-Ahram, 1990).

Center for Social Studies and Research of the Federation of Charitable Societies, *Dalil al-jama'iyyat al-khayriyyah* (Amman, 1985).

Daraghmah, Izzat, *Al-harakah al-nisa'iyyah fi filastin, 1903–1990* (Jerusalem: Diya' Center, 1991).

al-Din, Rislan Sharaf, "Al-din wa al-ahzab al-siyasiyyah al-diniyyah," *Al-din fi al-mujtama' al-'arabi* (Beirut: Center for the Studies of Arab Unity, 1990).

al-Fattash, Ibrahim, *Tarikh al-harakah al-niqabiyyah min sanat 1917 ila 1992* (Jerusalem: n.p., 1992).

General Federation of Trade Unions of Egypt, *Al-masikrahi al-tarikiyya fi khamsah wa thalathin 'aman* (Cairo: GFTUE, 1991).

al-Ghanushi, Rashid, *Al-hurriyyat al-'amah fi al-isalm* (Beirut: Center for the Studies of Arab Unity, 1993).

———, "Mustaqbal al-tayyar al-islami, *Minbar al-Sharq,* no. 1 (March 1992), pp. 3–32.

al-Ghazali, Salah, *Sour al-kuwait al-rabi'a,* vol. 3 (Kuwait, 1992).

al-Hamidi, Muhammad al-Hashimi, "Awlawiyyat muhimah fi daftar al-harakat al-islamiyyah: nahwa mithaq islami li al-'adl wa al-shura wa huquq al-insan," *Al-Mustaqbal al-Islami,* no. 2 (November 1991), pp. 19–21.

al-Hannachi, 'Abd al-Latif, "Niqash," *Al-mujtama' al-madani wa al-mashru' al-salafi* (Tunis: UGTT Publications, 1991), pp. 54–55.

Hawa, Sa'id, *Al-madkhal ila da'wat al-ikhwan al-muslimin bi-munasabat khamsin 'aman 'ala ta'sisiha* (Amman: Dar al-Arqam, 2d ed., 1979).

Hawrani, Yusuf, "Al-harakah al-niqabiyyah al-'ummaliyyah ila ayna?" *Al-Jadid,* 1/2 (1991), pp. 63–64.

al-Hay'ah al-'amma li Shu'un al-Matabi al Amiriyyah, *Dustur jumhuriyyat misr al-'arabiyyah* (Cairo: HASMA, 1991).

Hizb al-Ba'th al-'Arabi al-Ishtiraki, *Taqarir al-mu'tamar al-qutri al-thamin wa muqarraratihi* (Damascus, 1985).

al-Huwaydi, Fahmi, *Al-islam wa al-dimuqratiyyah* (Cairo: Markaz al-Ahram li al-Tarjamah wa al-Nahr, 1993).

Ibrahim, Saad Eddin, *Al-mujtama' al-madani wa al-tahawul al-dimuqrati fi al-watan al-'arabi* (Cairo: Ibn Khaldoun Center, 1992).

———, *Ta'ammulat fi mas'alat al-aqaliyat fi al-watan al-'arabi* (Cairo: Ibn Khaldoun/al-Sabah, 1992).

———, *Al-mujtama' al-madani wa al-tahawul al-dimuqrati fi al-watan al-'arabi* (Cairo: Markaz Ibn Khaldun, October 1991).

Isma'il, Mahmud, *Susiulujiah al-fikr al-islami* (Cairo: Maktabat Madbuli, 1988).

al-Janhani, al-Habib, "Al-sahwah al-islamiyyah fi bilad al-sham: Mithal suriyya," *Al-harakat al-islamiyyah al-mu'asirah fi al-watan al-'arabi* (Beirut: Center for the Studies of Arab Unity, 2d ed., 1989).

al-Jarbawi, 'Ali, *Waqfah naqdiyyah ma' tajrubat al-tanmiyyah al-filastiniyyah* (West Bank: Bir Zeit University, 1991), pp. 46–48.

———, *Al-intifadah wa al-qiyadat al-siyasiyyah fi al-diffah al-gharbiyyah wa qita' ghazzah, bahth fi al-nukhbah al-siyasiyyah* (Beirut: Dar al-Tali'ah, 1989).

Kawtharani, Wajih, *Al-sultah wa al-mujtama' wa al-'amal al-siyasi* (Beirut: Center for the Studies of Arab Unity, 1988).

Kerrou, Mohamed, "Hawla muqawalat al-mujtama' al-madani," *Utruhat,* no. 15 (1989), pp. 26–29.

———, "Al-muthakafun wa al-mujtama' al-madani fi tunis," *Al-Mustaqbal al-'Arabi* 10, no. 104 (1987): 46–60.

Khalidi, Salah A., *Sayyid Qutb, al-shahid al-hayy* ('Amman: Dar al-Firqan, 1983).

Kibi, Zuhayr, ed., *Abu Bakr al-Jassas, dirash fi fikratihi: bab al-ijtihad* (Beirut: Dar al-Muntakhab, 1993).

al-Kilani, Mohamed, "Al-mujtama' al-madani," in Tahir Labib et al., *Al-mujtama' al-madani* (Tunis: UGTT Publications, 1991), pp. 43–47.

Labib, Tahir, et al., *Al-mujtama' al-madani* (Tunis: UGTT Publications, 1991).

Madani, Abassi, *Azmat al-fikr al-hadith wa mubarrirat al-hal al-islami* (Algiers: Maktabat Rihab, 1989).

———, *Al-Naw'iyyah al-tarbawiyyah fi al-marahil al-ta'limiyyah fi al-bilad al-islamiyyah* (Riyadh, Saudi Arabia: Maktabat Duwalu al-Khalij, 1989).

———, *Al-Mushkilat al-tarbawiyyah fi al-bilad al-islamiyyah* (Batna, Algeria: Dar Rihab, 1986).

Mahfuz, Mohammed, "Usus al-mujtama' al-madani," *Al-mujtama' al-madani wa al-mashru'a al-salafi* (Tunis: UGTT Publications, 1991), pp. 31–53.

———, *Alladhina* zulimu (London: Riad al-Rayyis Books Ltd., 1988).

Mahmud, Ahmad Shawqi, *Al-tajribah al-dimuqratiyyah fi al-sudan* (Cairo: Alam al-Kutub, 1986).

Manea, Ilham M., *Al-ahzab wa al-tanthimat al-siyasiyyah fi al-yaman* (1948–1993) (Sana'a: Kitb al-Thawbit 2, 1994).

al-Mawardi, *Al-'ahkam al-sultaniyyah* (Cairo: 3d ed., 1973).

Messara, Antoine, "Al-mujtama' al-madani fi mujabahah nidham al-harb: al-hala al-lubnaniyyah," a paper presented at a conference in Giza, Egypt, 28–30 May 1992.

Morsi, Amin Taha, "Al-inqilab al-akhir fi ittihad al-'ummal," *Rose el-Youssef,* no. 3410 (Cairo, 18 October 1993).

al-Mu'assasah al-'Arabiyyah li al-Dirasat wa al-Nashr, *Suhayr salti al-tall, muqaddimat hawla qadiyat al-mar'ah wa al-harakah al-nisa'iyyah fi al-urdunn* (Beirut, 1985).

al-Muhami, Amir Salim, *Difa'an an haqq takwin al-jam'iyyat* (Cairo, 1992).

Muradh, Da'd, "Tajribat al-ittihad al-nisa', 1974–1981," *Al-Urdun al-Jadid* 7 (Spring 1986): 61–64.

al-Nabahani, Taqiy al-Din, *Al-takatul al-hizbi* (Jerusalem: n.p., 2d ed., 1953).

———, *Nizam al-hukm* (Jerusalem: Matba'at al-Thiryan, 1952).

PLO Research Center, *'Isa al-ahu'aybi, al-kiyaniyyah al-filastiniyyah: al-wa'i al-dhati wa al-tatawwur al-mu'assasati, 1947–1977* (Beirut, 1979).

al-Qadir, 'Abd, "Harakat siyassiyyah fi qita' ghazzah: 1948–1987," *Samid al-Iqtisadi* 2, no. 84 (1991): 30–46.

Qutb, Sayyid, *Al-salam al-'alami wa al-islam* (Beirut: Dar al-Shuruq, 7th ed., 1983).

———, *Ma'alim fi al-tariq* (Beirut: Dar al-Shuruq, 7th ed., 1980).

Rif'at, Rahma, "Al-Intihakat al-qanuniyyah wa al-idariyyah fi intikhbat 1991," *Nadwat al-harakah al-ummaliyyah al-misriyyah fi al-intikhabat al-niqabiyyah 'am 1991* (Cairo: Arab Research Center, December 1992).

Rizk, Y. L., *Misr al-madaniyyah* (Cairo: Tiba, 1993).

Sabella, Bernard, "Al-diffah al-gharbiyyah wa qita' ghazzah: as-sukkan wa al-ard," in *Al-mujtama' al-filastini fi al-diffah al-gharbiyyah wa qita' ghazzah,* Liza Taraki, ed. (Akka: Dar al-Aswar, 1990).

Saghiyyah, Hazim, "Ma'zufat al-mujtama' al-madani," *Al-Hayat,* Tayyarat Section, 18 September 1993, p. 4.

al-Said, Rifat, *Hasan al-Banna, mu'assis harakat al-ikhwan al-muslimin* (Beirut: Dar al-Tali'ah, 1981).

Sami', Salih Hasan, *Azmat al-hurriyyah al-siyasiyyah fi al-watan al-'arabi* (Cairo: Al-Zahra' li al-'I'lam al-'Arabi, 1988).

al-Sayyid, Mustapha Kamil, *Al-mujtama' wa al-siyasah fi misr: dawr jama'at al-masalih fi al-nizam al-siyasi al-misri* (Cairo: Dar al-Mustaqbal al-Arabi, 1983).

al-Sayyid, Radwan, *Mafahim al-jama'at fi al-islam* (Beirut: Dar al-Tanwir, 1984).

Shafiq, Munir, "Awlawiyyat amam al-ijtihad wa al-tajdid," *Al-ijtihad wa tajdid fi al-fir al-islami al-mu'asir* (Malta: Center for the Studies of the Muslim World, 1991).

al-Sharqi, Raufa Hassan, "Al-tanthimat al-ahliyyah al-yamaniyyah," Report to the Conference on Local Arab Organizations, sponsored by CIVICUS, Sana'a University (Sana'a, 1993).

Tamari, Salim, "Al-takhalluf wa afaq al-tanmiyyah fi al-diffah al-gharbiyyah wa qita' ghazzah al-muhtallayn," in *Al-mujtam'a al-filastini fi al-diffah al-gharbiyyah wa qita' ghazzah,* Liza Taraki, ed. (Akka: Dar al-Aswar, 1990).

al-Turabi, Hasan, "Awlawiyyat al-tayyar al-islami," *Minbar al-Sharq,* no. 1 (March 1992), pp. 21–26, 69–72, 81–82, 136–138, 167–169 and 198–199.

———, *Qadayah al-hurriyyah wa al-wahdah, al-shurah wa al-dimuqratiyyah, al-din wa al-fan* (Jiddah: Al-Dar al-Su'udiyyah li al-Nashr wa al-Tawzi', 1987).

al-Umari, Akram, *Al-mujtama' al-madani fi ahd al-nubuwah, khasa'isuhu wa tanzimatuhu al-'ula* (Madinah: Al-Majlis al-'Ilmi li-'Ihya' al-Turath al-Islami, 1983).

Yahya, Amin al-Hajj, *Al-'amal al-ijtima'i fi dhill al-intifadah* (Jerusalem, n.p., 1988).

Yemeni Organization for Defense of Rights and Liberties, *Al-munathamah al-yamaniyyah li al-difa'a 'an al-haqq wa al-huriyyah: al-nitham al-asasi,* booklet (Sana'a, 1992).

English-Language Sources

Abadan-Unat, Nermin, "Market Research and Public Opinion Polling in Turkey as an Agent of Social Change," in *Structural Change in Turkish Society,* Mübeccel Kıray, ed. (Bloomington, IN: Indiana University Turkish Studies 10, 1991), pp. 179–192.

———, "The Legal Status of Turkish Women," in *Women, Family and Social Change in Turkey,* Ferhunde Özbay, ed. (New York: UNESCO, 1990), pp. 13–27.

'Abbas, 'Ali 'Abdallah, "The National Islamic Front and the Politics of Education," in *Middle East Report,* no. 172 (September–October 1991).

'Abdallah, Ahmad, "Egypt's Islamists and the State," *Middle East Report,* no. 183 (July–August 1993), pp. 28–31.

Abir, Mordechai, *Saudi Arabia in the Oil Era* (Boulder, CO: Westview Press, 1988).

Abrahamian, Ervand, *Khemeinism: Essays on the Islamic Republic* (Berkeley: University of California Press, 1993).

————, *Radical Islam: The Iranian Mojahedin* (London: Tauris, 1989).

Abramowitz, Morton, "Dateline Ankara: Turkey After Ozal," *Foreign Policy* 91 (Summer 1993): 164–181.

Abu Ghazaleh, Adnan, "Arab Cultural Nationalism in Palestine During the British Mandate, *Journal of Palestine Studies* 1, no. 3 (Spring 1972): 37–63.

AbuKhalil, As'ad, "The Incoherence of Islamic Fundamentalism: Arab Islamic Thought at the End of the 20th Century," *Middle East Journal* 48, no. 4 (Autumn 1994): 677–694.

————, "The Study of Political Parties in the Arab World: The Case of Lebanon," *Journal of Asian and African Affairs* (Fall 1993), pp. 49–64.

————, "Toward the Study of Women and Politics in the Arab World: The Debate and the Reality," *Feminist Issues* 13, no. 1 (Spring 1993): 3–22.

————, "A Viable Partnership: Islam, Democracy, and the Arab World," *Harvard International Review* XV, no. 2 (Winter 1992–1993): 22–23, 65.

Abu-Rabi, Ibrahim M., "Islamic Resurgence in the Modern Arab World: Toward a Theoretical Appreciation," *Middle East Affairs Journal* 1, no. 2 (Winter 1993): 43–54.

Acar, Feride, "Women in the Ideology of Islamic Revivalism in Turkey: Three Islamic Women's Journals," in *Islam in Modern Turkey: Religion, Politics and Literature in a Secular State,* Richard Tapper, ed. (London: I. B. Tauris, 1991), pp. 280–303.

Adams, Charles, *Islam and Modernism in Egypt* (New York: Russell and Russell, 1986).

'Addi, Lahouari, "The Islamist Challenge: Religion and Modernity in Algeria," *Journal of Democracy* 3, no. 4 (October 1992): 75–84.

Afshar, Haleh, "Women, State and Ideology in Iran," *Third World Quarterly* 7, no. 2 (April 1985): 256–278.

Agassi, Joseph, *Between Faith and Nationality: Toward an Israeli National Identity* (Tel Aviv: Papyrus, 1993).

Ahmad, Feroz, "Politics and Islam in Modern Turkey," *Middle Eastern Studies* 27 (January 1991): 3–21.

————, "The Transition to Democracy in Turkey," *Third World Quarterly* 7, no. 2 (April 1985): 211–226.

Ahmed, Akbar S., *Postmodernism and Islam: Predicament and Promise* (New York: Routledge, 1992).

al-Ahsan, Sayed 'Aziz, "Economic Policy and Class Structure in Syria: 1958–1980," *International Journal of Middle East Studies* 16 (1984): 301–323.

Akhavi, Shahrough, "Shi'ism, Corporatism, and Rentierism in the Iranian Revolution," in *Comparing Muslim Societies: Knowledge and the State in a World Civilization,* Juan Cole, ed. (Ann Arbor: University of Michigan Press, 1992), pp. 261–293.

Akzin, Benjamin, "The Role of Parties in Israeli Democracy," in *Israel Social Structure,* Eisenstadt N. Samuel, et al., eds. (Jerusalem: Academon, 1966), pp. 111–156.

Alkan, Türker, "The National Salvation Party in Turkey," *Islam and Politics in the Modern Middle East,* Metin Heper and R. Israeli, eds. (London: Croom Helm, 1984), pp. 79–102.

Almond, Gabriel, "The Return to the State," *American Political Science Review* 82, no. 3 (September 1988): 853–901.

Alshayeji, 'Abdullah, "Kuwait at the Crossroads: The Quest for Democratization," *Middle East Insight* 8, no. 5 (May/June 1992): 41–46.

Alyushin, Alexey L., "The Paternalistic Tradition and Russia's Transition to Liberal Democracy," *Democratic Institutions,* vol. 1 (New York: Carnegie Council on Ethics and International Affairs).

Amin, Samir, "The Issue of Democracy in the Contemporary Third World," *Socialism and Democracy* 12 (January 1991): 83–104.

Amrane, Djamila, "Algeria: Anticolonial War," in *Female Soldiers—Combatants or Non-Combatants? Historical and Contemporary Perspectives,* Nancy Loring Goldman, ed. (Westport, CT: Greenwood Press, 1982), pp. 123–135.

Amuzegar, Jahngir, *Iran's Economy Under the Islamic Republic* (London: I. B. Tauris, 1993).

Anderson, Lisa, "Remaking the Middle East: The Prospects for Democracy and Stability," *Ethics and International Affairs* 6 (1992): 163–178.

———, "Absolutism and the Resilience of Monarchy in the Middle East," *Political Science Quarterly* 106, no. 1 (1991): 1–15.

———, "Liberalism in Northern Africa," *Current History* 89, no. 546 (April 1990): 145–148, 174–175.

———, "The State in the Middle East and North Africa," *Comparative Politics* 20, no. 1 (October 1987): 1–18.

———, *The State and Social Transformation in Tunisia and Libya* (Princeton: Princeton University Press, 1986).

Anderson, Perry, *Lineages of the Absolutist State* (London: Verso, 1974).

Anthony, John Duke, *Arab States of the Lower Gulf: People, Politics, Petroleum* (Washington, DC: The Middle East Institute, 1975).

Antonius, Rachad, and Qassal Samak, "Civil Society at the Pan-Arab Level? The Role of Non-Governmental Organizations," in *Arab Nationalism and the Future of the Arab World,* Hani A. Faris, ed. (Boston, MA: Association of Arab-American University Graduates, 1987).

Apter, David E., *Rethinking Development: Modernization, Dependency, and Postmodern Politics* (Newbury Park, CA: Sage, 1987).

Arat, Yeşim, "Women's Studies in Turkey: From Kemalism to Feminism," *New Perspectives on Turkey* 9 (1993): 119–134.

———, "Social Change and the 1983 Governing Elite in Turkey," *Structural Change in Turkish Society,* Mübeccel Kiray, ed. (Bloomington, IN: Indiana University Turkish Studies 10, 1991), pp. 163–178.

———, "Islamic Fundamentalism and Women in Turkey," *The Muslim World,* January 1990, pp. 17–23.

Arat, Zehra F., "Democracy and Economic Development: Modernization Theory Revisited," *Comparative Politics* 21, no. 1 (October 1988): 21–36.

Arato, Andrew, "Civil Society Against the State: Poland 1980–81," *Telos,* no. 47 (Spring 1981), pp. 23–47.

Arato, Andrew, and Jean Cohen, "Social Movements, Civil Society, and the Problem of Sovereignty," *Praxis International* 4, no. 3 (October 1984): 266–283.

Arian, Asher, and Michal Shamir, *The Elections in Israel, 1988* (Boulder, CO: Westview Press, 1988).

Arkoun, Mohammed, *Rethinking Islam: Common Questions, Uncommon Answers* (Boulder, CO: Westview Press, 1994).

Asad, Talal, "Religion and Politics: An Introduction," *Social Research* 59, no. 1 (Spring 1992): 3–16.

Ashraf, Ahmad, "Theocracy and Charisma: New Men of Power in Iran," *International Journal of Politics, Culture, and Society* 4 (1990).

Auda, Gehad, "Egypt's Uneasy Party Politics," *Journal of Democracy* 2, no. 2 (Spring 1991): 70–78.

Ayata, Sencer, "Traditional Sufi Orders on the Periphery: Kadiri and Nakşibendi Islam in Konya and Trabzon," in *Islam in Modern Turkey: Religion, Politics and Literature in a Secular State,* Richard Tapper, ed. (London: I. B. Tauris, 1991), pp. 223–253.

Ayubi, Nazih N., "Withered Socialism or Whether Socialism? The Radical Arab States as Populist-Corporatist Regimes," *Third World Quarterly* 13, no. 1 (1992): 89–105.

———, *Political Islam: Religion and Politics in the Arab World* (London and New York: Routledge, 1991).

Azari, Farah, ed., *Women of Iran: The Conflict with Fundamentalist Islam* (London: Ithaca Press, 1983).

Azarya, Victor, "Reordering State-Society Relations: Incorporation and Disengagement," in *The Precarious Balance: State and Society in Africa,* Donald Rothchild and Naomi Chazan, eds. (Boulder, CO: Westview Press, 1988), pp. 3–21.

al-Azmeh, Aziz, *Islams and Modernites* (London: Verso, 1993).

Badr, Gamal, "The Recent Impact of Islamic Religious Doctrine on Constitutional Law in the Middle East," in *The Islamic Impulse,* Barbara F. Stowasser, ed. (London and Sydney: Croom Helm, 1987).

Bahgat, Gawdat, "Democracy in the Middle East: The American Connection," *Studies in Conflict and Terrorism* 17 (1994): 87–96.

Baker, Raymond, *Sadat and After: Struggles for Egypt's Political Soul* (Cambridge: Harvard University Press, 1990).

Bakhash, Shaul, *The Reign of the Ayatollahs: Iran and the Islamic Revolution* (New York: Basic Books, 1984).

al-Banna, Hasan, *Memoirs of Hasan al-Banna Shaheed,* M. N. Shaikh, trans. (Karachi: International Islamic Publishers, 1981).

Banuazizi, 'Ali, "Political Factionalism and Societal Resistance in Iran," *Middle East Report* (forthcoming).

———, "Social-Psychological Approaches to Political Development," in *Understanding Political Development,* Myron Weiner and Samuel P. Huntington, eds. (Boston: Little, Brown, 1987), pp. 281–316.

Barghouthi, Mustafa, and Rita Giacaman, "The Emergence of an Infrastructure of Resistance: The Case of Health," in *Intifada: Palestine at the Crossroads,* Jamal R. Nassar and Roger Heacock, eds. (New York: Praeger Publishers, 1990), pp. 207–226.

Barnett, Michael, "Institutions, Roles, and Disorder: The Case of the Arab States System," *International Studies Quarterly* 37 (1993): 371–296.

Batatu, Hanna, *The Old Social Classes and the Revolutionary Movements of Iraq* (Princeton, NJ: Princeton University Press, 1978).

Bayart, Jean-François, "Civil Society in Africa," in *Political Domination in Africa: Reflections on the Limits of Power,* Patrick Chabal, ed. (London: Cambridge University Press, 1986), pp. 109–125.

Bayat, Assef, *Workers and Revolution in Iran: A Third World Experience of Workers' Control* (London: Zed, 1987).

Bayat, Mangol, "The Iranian Revolution of 1978–79: Fundamentalist or Modern?" *The Middle East Journal* 37, no. 1 (Winter 1983): 30–42.

Beblawi, Hazem, and Giacomo Luciani, eds., *The Rentier State* (London: Croom Helm, 1987).

Bechtold, Peter, *Politics in the Sudan: Parliamentary and Military Rule in an Emerging African Nation* (New York: Praeger, 1976).

Becker, David G., Jeff Frieden, Sayre P. Schatz, and Richard L. Sklar,

Postimperialism: International Capitalism and Development in the Late Twentieth Century (Boulder, CO: Lynne Rienner, 1993).

Beinen, Joel, and Zachary Lockman, *Workers on the Nile: Nationalism, Communism, Islam and the Egyptian Working Class, 1882–1954* (Princeton: Princeton University Press, 1987).

Bekkar, Rabia, "Taking Up Space in Tlemcen: The Islamist Occupation of Urban Algeria," *Middle East Report*, no. 179 (November/December 1992), pp. 11–15.

Bell, Daniel, "American Exceptionalism Revisited: The Role of Civil Society," *The Public Interest*, no. 95 (Spring 1989), pp. 38–56.

Bellin, Eva, "Civil Society in Formation: Tunisia," in *Civil Society in the Middle East*, vol. 1, Augustus Richard Norton, ed. (Leiden: E. J. Brill Publishers, 1994), pp. 120–147.

———, "Civil Society: Effective Tool of Analysis for Middle East Politics?" *PS: Political Science & Politics*, September 1994, pp. 509–510.

Ben-Eliezer, Uri, "The Meaning of Political Participation in a Nonliberal Democracy: The Israeli Experience," *Comparative Politics* 25, no. 4 (July 1993): 397–412.

Berger, Peter L., "The Uncertain Triumph of Democratic Capitalism," *Journal of Democracy* 3, no. 3 (July 1992): 7–16.

Bernhard, Michael, "Civil Society and Democratic Transition in East Central Europe," *Political Science Quarterly* 108, no. 2 (Summer 1993): 307–326.

Bianchi, Robert, *Unruly Corporatism: Associational Life in Twentieth-Century Egypt* (New York: Oxford University Press, 1989).

———, "Interest Group Politics in the Third World," *Third World Quarterly* 8, no. 2 (April 1986): 507–539.

Binder, Leonard, *Islamic Liberalism* (Chicago: University of Chicago Press, 1988).

Birnbaum, Karl E., "Civil Society and Government Policy in a New Europe," *The World Today* 47, no. 5 (May 1991): 84–85.

Bisan Center for Research and Development, *Directory of Palestinian Women's Organizations* (Ramallah, West Bank: Women's Studies Committee, 1993).

Blaney, David L., and Mustaph Kamal Pasha, "Civil Society and Democracy in the Third World: Ambiguities and Historical Possibilities," *Studies in Comparative International Development* 28, no. 1 (Spring 1993): 3–23.

Bligh, Alexander, "The Saudi Religious Elite (Ulama) as Participant in the Political System of the Kingdom," *International Journal of Middle East Studies* 17, no. 1 (February 1985): 37–50.

Bobbio, Norberto, *Democracy and Dictatorship: The Nature and Limits of State Power* (Minneapolis: University of Minnesota Press, 1989).

Boulding, Elise, ed., *Building Peace in the Middle East: Challenges for States and Civil Society* (Boulder, CO: Lynne Rienner Publishers, in association with the International Peace Research Association, 1994).

Brand, Laurie A., *Jordan's International Relations: The Political Economy of Alliance-Making* (New York: Columbia University Press, 1995).

———, "'In the Beginning Was the State . . .': The Quest for Civil Society in Jordan," in *Civil Society in the Middle East*, vol. 1, Augustus Richard Norton, ed. (Leiden: E. J. Brill Publishers, 1994), pp. 148–185.

———, *Palestinians in the Arab World: Institution Building and the Search for State* (New York: Columbia University Press, 1988).

Bratton, Michael, "Beyond the State: Civil Society and Associational Life in Africa," *World Politics* 41, no. 3 (April 1989): 407–430.

Bromley, Simon, *Rethinking Middle East Politics* (Austin: University of Texas Press, 1994).

Brumberg, Daniel, "Islam, Elections and Reform in Algeria," *Journal of Democracy* 2, no. 1 (Winter 1992): 58–71.

———, "An Arab Path to Democracy?" *Journal of Democracy* 1, no. 4 (Fall 1990): 120–125.

Brynen, Rex, "Economic Crisis and Post-Rentier Democratization in the Arab World: The Case of Jordan," *Canadian Journal of Political Science* XXV, no. 1 (March 1992): 69–97.

Buchan, James, "Secular and Religious Opposition in Saudi Arabia," in *State, Society and Economy in Saudi Arabia,* Tim Niblock, ed. (London: Croom Helm, 1982).

Bujra, 'Abdalla S., *The Politics of Stratification: A Study of Political Change in a South Arabian Town* (Oxford: Oxford University Press, 1971).

Burgat, Francois, and William Dowell, *The Islamist Movement in North Africa* (Austin: University of Texas Press, 1993).

Burrows, Robert D., "The Yemen Arab Republic's Legacy and Yemeni Unification," *Arab Studies Quarterly* 14, no. 4 (Fall 1992): 41–68.

Butterworth, Charles E., ed., *Political Islam, ANNALS,* American Academy of Political and Social Science, no. 524 (November 1992).

———, "State and Authority in Arabic Political Thought," in *The Foundations of the Arab State,* Ghassan Salamé, ed. (London: Croom Helm, 1987), pp. 91–111.

Calhoun, Craig, ed., *Habermas and the Public Sphere* (Cambridge, MA: MIT Press, 1993).

Cantori, Louis J., ed., "Democratization in the Middle East," *American-Arab Affairs,* no. 36 (Spring 1991), pp. 1–51.

Carapico, Sheila, "Yemen Between Civility and Civil War," in *Civil Society in the Middle East,* vol. 2, Augustus Richard Norton, ed. (Leiden, the Netherlands: E. J. Brill Publishers, 1995).

———, "Elections and Mass Politics in Yemen," *Middle East Report,* no. 185 (November–December 1993), pp. 2–6.

———, "Women and Public Participation in Yemen," *Middle East Report,* no. 173 (November–December 1991), p. 15.

Carnoy, Martin, *The State and Political Theory* (Princeton, NJ: Princeton University Press, 1984).

Caton, Steven C., "Anthropological Theories of Tribe and State Formation in the Middle East: Ideology and the Semiotics of Power," in *Tribes and State Formation in the Middle East,* Philip Khoury and J. Kostiner, eds. (Berkeley: University of California Press, 1990), pp. 74–108.

Chatterjee, Partha, "A Response to Taylor's 'Modes of Civil Society,'" in *Public Culture* 3 (1990): 119–132.

Chaudhry, Kiren Aziz, "The Myths of the Market and the Common History of Late Developers," *Politics and Society* 21, no. 3 (September 1993): 245–274.

———, "The Price of Wealth: Business and State in Labor Remittance and Oil Economies," *International Organization* 43 (Winter 1989).

Chazan, Naomi, "Africa's Democratic Challenge," *World Policy Journal* 9, no. 2 (Spring 1992): 279–307.

Chehabi, H. E., *Iranian Politics and Religious Modernism: The Liberation Movement of Iran Under the Shah and Khomeini* (Ithaca, NY: Cornell University Press, 1990).

Chilcote, Ronald H., *Theories of Development and Underdevelopment* (Boulder, CO: Westview Press, 1984).

Christelow, Allan, "Ritual, Culture and Politics of Islamic Reformism in Algeria," *Middle Eastern Studies* 23, no. 3 (July 1987): 255–273.

Cigar, Norman, "Islam and the State in South Yemen: The Uneasy Coexistence," *Middle Eastern Studies* 26, no. 2 (April 1990): 185–203.

Cobban, Helena, *The Palestinian Liberation Organization: People, Power and Politics* (New York: Cambridge University Press, 1984).

Cohen, Amnon, *Political Parties in the West Bank Under the Jordanian Regime, 1949–1967* (Ithaca, NY: Cornell University Press, 1982).

Cohen, Jean L., *Class and Civil Society: The Limits of Marxian Critical Theory* (Amherst: University of Massachusetts Press, 1982).

Cohen, Jean L., and Andrew Arato, *Civil Society and Political Theory* (Cambridge, MA: MIT Press, 1992).

Cole, Juan Ricardo, *Colonialism and Revolution in the Middle East: Social and Cultural Origins of Egypt's 'Urabi Movement* (Princeton, NJ: Princeton University Press, 1993).

Collings, Deirdre, ed., *Reconstruction, Rehabilitation and Reconciliation in the Middle East: The View from Civil Society* (report from a workshop of the same name held in Ottawa, Canada, June 1993).

Crone, Patricia, and Martin Hinds, *God's Caliph: Religious Authority in the First Century of Islam* (Cambridge: Cambridge University Press, 1980).

Crystal, Jill, "Civil Society in the Arab Gulf States," in *Civil Society in the Middle East*, vol. 2, Augustus Richard Norton, ed. (Leiden, the Netherlands: E. J. Brill Publishers, 1995).

———, "The Human Rights Movement in the Arab World," *Human Rights Quarterly* 16 (August 1994).

———, "Authoritarianism and Its Adversaries in the Arab World," *World Politics* 46, no. 2 (January 1994): 262–289.

———, *Kuwait, The Transformation of an Oil State* (Boulder, CO: Westview Press, 1992).

———, *Oil and Politics in the Gulf: Rulers and Merchants in Kuwait and Qatar* (New York: Cambridge University Press, 1990).

Dabashi, Hamid, *Authority in Islam* (New Brunswick, NJ: Transaction Publishers, 1989).

Dahl, Robert, "A Democratic Dilemma: System Effectiveness Versus Citizen Participation," *Political Science Quarterly* 109, no. 1 (Winter 1994): 23–34.

———, *Democracy and Its Critics* (New Haven, CT: Yale University Press, 1989).

———, "Governments and Political Opposition," in *Political Science, Scope and Theory* (Handbook of Political Science, Volume 3), Fred Greenstein and Nelson Polsby, eds. (New York: Addison-Wesley, 1975), pp. 115–122.

Dahrendorf, Ralf, *Reflections on the Revolution in Europe in a Letter Intended to Have Been Sent to a Gentleman in Warsaw* (New York: Times Books, 1990; London: Chatto and Windus, 1990).

———, *The Modern Social Conflict: An Essay on the Politics of Liberty* (New York: Weidenfeld and Nicholson, 1988).

Dawisha, Adeed, "Power, Participation and Legitimacy in the Arab World" *World Policy Journal* III, no. 3 (Summer 1986): 517–534.

Dekmejian, R. Hrair, "The Rise of Political Islamism in Saudi Arabia," *Middle East Journal* 48, no. 4 (Autumn 1994): 627–643.

Delacroix, Jacques, "The Distributive State in the World System," *Studies in Comparative International Development* 15 (1980).

Denoeux, Guilain, *Urban Unrest in the Middle East: A Comparative Study of Informal Networks in Egypt, Iran and Lebanon* (Albany, NY: SUNY Press, 1993).

Dessouki, Ali Hillal, "The Unfinished Revolution: The Postwar Arab World," *Journal of Democracy* 2, no. 3 (Summer 1991).

——, "The Shift in Egypt's Migration Policy: 1952–1978," *Middle Eastern Studies* no. 18 (1983): 53–68.

Detalle, Renaud, "The Yemeni Elections Up Close," *Middle East Report,* no. 185 (November–December 1993), pp. 8–12.

Diamond, Larry, "Rethinking Civil Society: Toward Democratic Consolidation," *Journal of Democracy* 5, no. 3 (July 1994): 3–17.

——, ed., *Political Culture and Democracy in Developing Countries* (Boulder, CO: Lynne Rienner Publishers, 1993).

——, "Promoting Democracy," *Foreign Policy* 87 (Summer 1992): 25–46.

——, "Three Paradoxes of Democracy," *Journal of Democracy* 1, no. 3 (Summer 1990): 48–60.

Diamond, Larry, Juan J. Linz, and Seymour Martin Lipset, eds., *Politics in Developing Countries: Comparing Experiences with Democracy* (Boulder, CO: Lynne Rienner Publishers, 1990).

——, *Democracy in Developing Countries* (Boulder, CO: Lynne Rienner Publishers, 1989).

——, "Building and Sustaining Democratic Government in Developing Countries: Some Tentative Findings," *World Affairs* 150, no. 1 (Summer 1987): 5–19.

Diamond, Larry, and Marc Plattner, eds., *The Global Resurgence of Democracy* (Baltimore, MD: The Johns Hopkins University Press, 1993).

Di Palma, Giuseppe, "Legitimation from the Top to Civil Society: Politico-Cultural Change in Eastern Europe," *World Politics* 44, no. 1 (October 1991): 9–80.

——, *To Craft Democracies: An Essay on Democratic Transitions* (Berkeley: University of California Press, 1990).

Dixon, William, "Democracy and the Political Settlement of International Conflict," *American Political Science Review* 88, no. 1 (March 1994): 314–332.

Doan, Rebecca Miles, "Class Differentiation and the Informal Sector in Amman, Jordan," *International Journal of Middle East Studies* 24, no. 1 (February 1992): 27–38.

Dor, Avi, "Can 'One Country, Two Governments' Resolve the Israeli-Palestinian Conflict? Some Second Thoughts," *Journal of Policy Analysis and Management* 8, no. 4 (1989): 668–669.

Doron, Gideon, "Two Civil Societies and One State: Jews and Arabs in the State of Israel," in *Civil Society in the Middle East,* vol. 2, Augustus Richard Norton, ed. (Leiden, the Netherlands: E. J. Brill Publishers, 1995).

Doron, Gideon, and Giora Goldberg, "No Big Deal: Democratization of the Nominating Process," in *The Elections in Israel: 1988,* Asher Arian and Michal Shamir, eds. (Boulder, CO: Westview Press, 1990).

Doron, Gideon, and Barry Kay, "Electoral Reforms in Israel," in *The Elections in Israel: 1992,* Asher Arian and Michal Shamir, eds. (Syracuse, NY: University of Syracuse Press, 1994).

Doron, Gideon, and Boaz Tamir, "The Electoral Cycle: A Political Economic Perspective," *Crossroads* 10 (Spring 1983): 141–163.

Dowty, Alan, "The Use of Emergency Powers in Israel," *Middle East Review* 21 (1988): 34–46.

Doyle, Michael W., "Liberalism and World Politics," *American Political Science Review* 80 (December 1986).

———, "Kant, Liberal Legacies, and Foreign Affairs, Part 2," *Philosophy & Public Affairs* 12 (Fall 1983): 323–353.

———, "Kant, Liberal Legacies, and Foreign Affairs, Part 1," *Philosophy & Public Affairs* 12 (Summer 1983): 205–235.

Dresch, Paul, "Tribalism and Democracy," *Chroniques Yemenites* (Sana'a, 1994).

———, *Tribes, Government, and History in Yemen* (Oxford: Oxford University Press, 1989).

Dunn, Michael C., "Revivalist Islam and Democracy: Thinking About the Algerian Quandary," *Middle East Policy* 1, no. 2 (1992): 16–22.

Eckstein, Harry, "A Culturalist Theory of Political Change," *American Political Science Review* 82, no. 3 (September 1988), pp. 789–804.

Eickelman, Christine, *Women and Community in Oman* (New York: New York University Press, 1984).

Eickelman, Dale F., "The Re-Imagination of the Middle East: Political and Academic Frontiers (1991 Presidential Address)," *Middle East Studies Association Bulletin* 26, no. 1 (July 1992): 3–12.

———, "Mass Higher Education and the Religious Imagination in Contemporary Arab Societies," *American Ethnologist* 19, no. 4 (1992): 643–655.

———, "Oman's Next Generation: Challenges and Prospects," in *Crosscurrents in the Gulf,* Richard Sindelar and J. E. Peterson, eds. (London: Routledge, 1988).

———, "Changing Perceptions of State Authority: Morocco, Egypt, and Oman," in *The Foundations of the Arab State,* Ghassan Salamé, ed. (London: Croom Helm, 1987), pp. 177–204.

———, "Kings and People: Oman's State Consultative Council," *Middle East Journal* 38, no. 1 (Winter 1984): 51–71.

Eisenstadt, N. Samuel, *Israeli Society* (London: Weidenfeld and Nicolson, 1967).

Ember, Carol R., Ember, Melvin, and Bruce M. Russett, "Peace Between Participatory Polities: A Cross Cultural Test of the 'Democracies Rarely Fight Each Other' Hypothesis," *World Politics* 44, no. 4 (July 1992): 573–599.

Entelis, John, "Civil Society and the Authoritarian Temptation in Algerian Politics: Islamist Democracy vs. the Centralized State," in *Civil Society in the Middle East,* vol. 2, Augustus Richard Norton, ed. (Leiden, the Netherlands: E. J. Brill Publishers, 1995).

———, "The Crisis of Authoritarianism in North Africa: The Case of Algeria," *Problems of Communism* XLI (May–June 1992): 71–81.

———, "Algeria Under Chadli: Liberalization Without Democratization or, Perestroika, Yes; Glasnost, No!" *Middle East Insight* 6, no. 3 (1988): 47–64.

———, "Oil Wealth and the Prospects for Democratization in the Arabian Peninsula: The Case of Saudi Arabia," in *Arab Oil: Impact on the Arab Countries and Global Implications,* Naiem A. Sherbiny and Mark A. Tessler, eds. (New York: Praeger Publishers, 1976), pp. 77–111.

Entelis, John, and Phillip Naylor, eds., *State and Society in Algeria* (Boulder, CO: Westview Press, 1992).

Ergüder, Üstun, "Decentralization of Local Government and Turkish Political Culture," in *Democracy and Local Government: Istanbul in the 1980s,* Metin Heper, ed. (Atlantic Highlands, NJ: Eothen Press, 1987).

Escher, Anton, "Private Business and Trade in the Region of Yabroud, Syria" (unpublished paper presented at the Middle East Studies Association annual meeting, 1990).

Esposito, John L., *The Islamic Threat: Myth or Reality?* (New York: Oxford University Press, 1992).

Esposito, John L., and James P. Piscatori, "Democratization and Islam," *Middle East Journal* 45, no. 3 (Summer 1991): 427–440.

Esseghir, Mohamed, "Algeria: International Silence over Human Rights Abuses and Torture," *Inquiry* 2, no. 7 (March/April 1993): 27, 62.

Evans, Peter B., "Foreign Capital and the Third World State," in *Understanding Political Development,* Myron Weiner and Samuel P. Huntington, eds. (Boston, MA: Little, Brown, 1987), pp. 319–352.

———, Dietrich Rueschemeyer, and Theda Skocpol, *Bringing the State Back In* (Cambridge: Cambridge University Press, 1985).

al-Falah, Noura, "Kuwait: God's Will and the Process of Socialization," in *Sisterhood Is Global,* Robin Morgan, ed. (New York: Doubleday, 1981).

Fandy, Mahmoun, "Egypt's Islamic Groups: Regional Revenge?" *Middle East Journal* 48, no. 4 (Autumn 1994): 607–625.

Farsoun, Samih K., "Class Structure and Social Change in the Arab World: 1995," in *The Next Arab Decade: Alternative Futures,* Hisham Sharabi, ed. (Boulder, CO: Westview Press, 1988), pp. 221–238.

Fergany, Nader, "A Characterization of the Employment Problem in Egypt," in *Employment and Structural Adjustment: Egypt in the 1990s,* Heba Handoussa and Gillian Potter, eds. (Cairo: American University in Cairo Press for the International Labour Organization, 1991).

Ferguson, Adam, *An Essay on the History of Civil Society* (Edinburgh: Printed for A. Millar and T. Caddel, London, and A. Kincaid and J. Bell, Edinburgh, 1767).

Fernea, Elizabeth Warcock, and Mary Evelyn Hocking, *The Struggle for Peace: Israelis and Palestinians* (Austin: University of Texas Press, 1992).

Ferrarotti, Franco, "Civil Society as a Polyarchic Form: The City," *International Journal of Politics, Culture and Society* 6, no. 1 (1992): 23–37.

Foran, John, *Fragile Resistance: Social Transformation of Iran from 1500 to the Revolution* (Boulder, CO: Westview Press, 1993).

Frentzel-Zagorska, Janina, "Civil Society in Poland and Hungary," *Soviet Studies* 42, no. 4 (1990): 759–777.

Frieden, Jeffrey, "International Finance and the Third World," *MERIP Reports,* no. 117 (1983), pp. 3–11.

———, "Third World Indebted Industrialization," *International Organization* 35, no. 3 (1981): 407–431.

Friedl, Erika, "Sources of Female Power in Iran," in *In the Eye of the Storm,* Mahnaz Afkhami and Erika Friedl, eds. (London: I. B. Tauris, 1994).

Frohlich, Norman, and Joe Oppenheimer, *Modern Political Economy* (Englewood Cliffs, NJ: Prentice Hall, 1978).

Fuller, Graham, "Respecting Regional Realities," *Foreign Policy* 83 (Summer 1991): 39–46.

Gasiorowski, Mark, "The Failure of Reform in Tunisia," *Journal of Democracy* 3, no. 4 (October 1992): 85–97.

Gause, F. Gregory, *Oil Monarchies: Domestic and Security Challenges in the Arab Gulf States* (New York: Council on Foreign Relations, 1994).

———, "Sovereignty, Statecraft, and Stability in the Middle East," *Journal of International Affairs* 45, no. 2 (Winter 1992): 441–469.

Gellner, Ernest, *Conditions of Liberty: Civil Society and Its Rivals* (New York: Allen Lane, The Penguin Press, 1994).
——, *Post-Modernism, Reason and Religion* (London: Routledge, 1992).
——, "Civil Society in Historical Context," *International Social Science Journal* 43 (August 1991): 495–510.
——, *Culture, Identity and Politics* (Cambridge, MA: Cambridge University Press, 1988).
Ghabra, Shafeeq, "Kuwait: Elections and Issues of Democratization in a Middle Eastern State," *Digest of Middle East Studies* 2, no. 1 (Winter 1993): 1–17.
——, "Voluntary Associations in Kuwait: The Foundation of a New System," *Middle East Journal* 45, no. 2 (Spring 1991): 199–215.
Giacaman, Rita, and Penny Johnson, "Palestinian Women: Building Barricades and Breaking Barriers," in *Intifada: The Palestinian Uprising Against Israeli Occupation,* Zachary Lockman and Joel Beinin, eds. (Boston: South End Press, 1989), pp. 155–169.
Gillies, David, and G. Schmitz, *The Challenge of Democratic Development: Sustaining Democratization in Developing Countries* (Ottawa: The North-South Institute, 1992).
Gilsenan, Michael, *Recognizing Islam: Religion and Society in the Modern Middle East* (London: I. B. Taurus & Co., 1994).
Goldberg, Ellis, Resat Kasaba, and Joel Migdal, eds., *Rules and Rights in the Middle East: Democracy, Law and Society* (Seattle: University of Washington Press, 1993).
Goldberg, Ellis, "Private Goods, Public Wrongs, and Civil Society in Some Medieval Arab Theory and Practice," in *Rules and Rights in the Middle East: Democracy, Law and Society,* Ellis Goldberg, Resat Kasaba, and Joel Migdal, eds. (Seattle: University of Washington Press, 1993), pp. 248–271.
——, "The Foundations of State-Labor Relations in Contemporary Egypt," *Comparative Politics* 24, no. 2 (January 1992): 147–161.
Göle, Nilüfer, "Authoritarian Secularism and Islamic Participation: The Case of Turkey," in *Civil Society in the Middle East,* vol. 2, Augustus Richard Norton, ed. (Leiden, the Netherlands: E. J. Brill Publishers, 1995).
——, "Toward an Autonomization of Politics and Civil Society in Turkey," in *Politics in the Third Turkish Republic,* Metin Heper and Ahmet Evin, eds. (Boulder, CO: Westview Press, 1994), pp. 213–222.
——, "Engineers and the Emergence of a Technicist Identity," in *Turkey and the West: Changing Political and Cultural Identities,* Metin Heper, Ayse Oncu, and Heinz Kramer, eds. (London: I. B. Tauris, 1993).
Graham, Douglas F., *Saudi Arabia Unveiled* (Dubuque, IA: Kendall/Hunt Publishing, 1991).
Gramsci, Antonio, *Selections from the Prison Notebooks,* Quintin Hoare and Geoffrey Nowell Smith, eds. and trans. (London: Lawrence and Wishart, 1971).
Green, Jerrold D., "Political Reform and Regime Stability in the Post-War Gulf," *Studies in Conflict and Terrorism* 16 (1993): 9–23.
——, "Islam, Religiopolitics, and Social Change," *Comparative Studies in Society and History* 27, no. 2 (April 1985): 312–322.
Gülfidan, Şebnem, *Big Business and the State in Turkey: The Case of TÜSIAD* (Istanbul: Boğaziçi University Press, 1993).
Habermas, Jürgen, *The Structural Transformation of the Public Sphere: An Inquiry into a Category of Bourgeois Society* (Cambridge, MA: MIT Press, 1989).

————, *Theory of Communicative Action,* vols. 1 and 2 (Boston: Beacon Press, 1984).

Hadar, Leon T., "What Green Peril?" *Foreign Affairs* 72, no. 2 (Spring 1993): 28–42.

Haddad, Mahmoud, "The Rise of Arab Nationalism Reconsidered," *International Journal of Middle East Studies* 26, no. 2 (May 1994): 201–222.

al-Haddad, Mohammad, *The Effect of Detribalization and Sedentarization on the Socio-Economic Structure of the Tribes of the Arabian Peninsula: Ajman Tribe as a Case Study,* Ph.D. dissertation, University of Kansas, 1981.

Haeri, Shahla, "Temporary Marriage: An Islamic Discourse on Female Sexuality in Iran," in *In the Eye of the Storm: Women in the Post-Revolutionary Iran,* Mahnaz Afkhami and Erika Friedl, eds. (London: I. B. Tauris, 1994).

————, *Law of Desire: Temporary Marriage in Shi'i Iran* (Syracuse, NY: Syracuse University Press, 1989).

Hagopian, Frances, "After Regime Change: Authoritarian Legacies, Political Representation, and the Democratic Future of South America," *World Politics* 45 (April 1993): 464–500.

————, "Arab Intellectual Discourse on Civil Society: Regional Models," paper presented at a conference entitled, Prospects for Democracy in the Arab World, Simmons College, Boston, MA, April 1993.

al-Haj, Majid, and Henry Rosenfeld, "The Emergence of an Indigenous Political Framework in Israel: The National Committee of Arab Local Authorities," *Asian and African Studies* 23 (1990): 205–244.

Hale, Sondra, "The Rise of Islam and Women of the National Islamic Front in Sudan," *Review of African Political Economy,* no. 554 (1992).

Halperin, Manfred, *The Politics of Social Change in the Middle East and the Arab World* (Princeton, NJ: Princeton University Press, 1962).

Halperin, Morton H., and David J. Scheffer with Patricia L. Small, *Self-Determination in the New World Order* (Washington, DC: Carnegie Endowment for International Peace, 1992).

Hanf, Theodor, *Coexistence in Wartime Lebanon: Decline of a State and Rise of a Nation* (London: Centre for Lebanese Studies and I. B. Tauris, 1993).

Hardin, Russell, "Norms of Exclusion and Difference," Working Paper #39, Russell Sage Foundation (May 1993).

Harik, Iliya, "Rethinking Civil Society: Pluralism in the Arab World," *Journal of Democracy* 5, no. 3 (July 1994): 43–56.

Harik, Judith P., and Hilal Khashan, "Lebanon's Divisive Democracy: The Parliamentary Elections of 1992," *Arab Studies Quarterly* 15, no. 1 (Winter 1993): 41–59.

Hatem, Mervat, "Egyptian Discourses on Gender and Political Liberalization: Do Secularist and Islamist Views Really Differ?" *Middle East Journal* 48, no. 4 (Autumn 1994): 661–676.

————, "Egypt's Middle Class in Crisis: The Sexual Division of Labor," *Middle East Journal* 42, no. 3 (Summer 1988): 407–422.

Hegel, Georg Wilhelm Friedrich, *Philosophy of Right* (London: Oxford University Press, 1967).

Heper, Metin, "The Strong State as a Problem for the Consolidation of Democracy: Turkey and Germany Compared," *Comparative Political Studies* 25, no. 2 (July 1992): 169–194.

————, "Political Modernization as Reflected in Bureaucratic Change: The Turkish Bureaucracy and a 'Historical Bureaucratic Empire' Tradition," *International Journal of Middle Eastern Studies* 7 (1976): 507–521.

Hermassi, Mohamed Abdelbaki, "Islam, Democracy, and the Challenge of Political

Change," in Yehuda Mirsky and Matt Abrens, eds., *Democracy in the Middle East: Defining the Challenge* (Washington, DC: The Washington Institute, 1993), pp. 41–52.

————, "Notes on Civil Society in Tunisia," a paper presented at a conference on Civil Society in the Arab World, Giza, Egypt, 28–30 May 1992.

————, *Society and State in the Arab Maghreb* (Beirut: Center for Arab Unity Studies, 1987).

————, *Leadership and National Development in North Africa: A Comparative Study* (Berkeley: University of California Press, 1970).

al-Hibri, 'Azizah Y., *Islamic Constitutionalism and the Concept of Democracy* (Washington, DC: American Muslim Foundation, 1992).

Hicks, Neil, and Ghanim al-Najjar, "The Utility of Tradition: Civil Society in Kuwait," in *Civil Society in the Middle East,* vol. 1, Augustus Richard Norton, ed. (Leiden: E. J. Brill Publishers, 1994), pp. 186–213.

Hiltermann, Joost, *Behind the Intifida: Labor and Women's Movements in the Occupied Territories* (Princeton, NJ: Princeton University Press, 1992).

Hinnebusch, Raymond A., "State, Civil Society, and Political Change in Syria," in *Civil Society in the Middle East,* vol. 1, Augustus Richard Norton, ed. (Leiden: E. J. Brill Publishers, 1994), pp. 214–242.

————, "State and Civil Society in Syria," *Middle East Journal* 47, no. 2 (Spring 1993): 241–257.

————, *Authoritarian Power and State Formation in Ba'thist Syria: Army, Party and Peasant* (Boulder, CO: Westview Press, 1990).

Hooglund, Eric, "Iranian Populism and Political Change in the Gulf," *Middle East Report,* no. 194 (January–February 1992), pp. 19–21.

Hopkins, Nicholas, "Class and State in Rural Arab Communities," in *Beyond Coercion,* Adeed Dawisha and I. William Zartman, eds. (London: Croom Helm, 1988).

Horowitz, Dan, "Before the State: Communal Politics in Palestine Under the Mandate," in *The Israeli State and Society,* Kimmerling Baruch, ed. (Albany: State University of New York Press, 1989), pp. 28–65.

Hourani, Albert, *History of the Arab People* (Cambridge, MA: Harvard University Press, 1990).

Hourani, Hani, et al., *The Islamic Action Front Party* (Amman: Al-Urdun al-Jadid, 1993).

Huber, Evelyn, Dietrich Rueschemeyer, and John D. Stephens, "The Impact of Economic Development on Democracy," *Journal of Economic Perspectives* 7, no. 3 (Summer 1993): 71–85.

Hudson, Michael C., "Democracy and Foreign Policy in the Arab World," *The Beirut Review,* no. 4 (Fall 1992), pp. 3–28.

————, "After the Gulf War: Prospects for Democratization in the Arab World," *Middle East Journal* 45, no. 3 (Summer 1991): 407–427.

————, "Democratization and the Problem of Legitimacy in Middle East Politics," 1987 MESA Presidential Address, *Middle East Studies Association Bulletin* 22, no. 2 (December 1988): 157–171.

————, "State, Society and Legitimacy: An Essay on Arab Political Prospects in the 1990s," in *The Next Decade: Alternative Futures,* Hisham Sharabi (Boulder, CO: Westview Press, 1988), pp. 22–37.

————, *Arab Politics: The Search for Legitimacy* (New Haven, CT: Yale University Press, 1980).

Huntington, Samuel P., "Clash of Civilizations?" *Foreign Affairs* 72, no. 3 (Summer 1993): 22–49.

——, *Political Order in Changing Societies* (New Haven, CT: Yale University Press, 1968).

——, "Democracy's Third Wave," *Journal of Democracy* 2, no. 2 (April 1991): 12–34.

——, "The Goals of Development," in *Understanding Political Development,* Myron Weiner and Samuel P. Huntington, eds. (Boston: Little, Brown, 1966), pp. 3–32.

al-Husseini, Ishaq Musa, *Moslem Brethren* (Beirut: Khayat's College Book, 1956).

Ibn Khaldoun Center, *Grass-Roots Participation and Development in Egypt* (a study commissioned by UNICEF, UNDP, and UNFPA: Cairo, 1993).

Ibrahim, Saad Eddin, "Civil Society and Prospects for Democratization in the Arab World," in *Civil Society in the Middle East,* vol. 1, Augustus Richard Norton, ed. (Leiden: E. J. Brill Publishers, 1994), pp. 27–54.

——, "Crises, Elites, and Democratization in the Arab World," *Middle East Journal* 47, no. 2 (Spring 1993): 292–305.

Isaac, Jeffrey, "Civil Society and the Spirit of Revolt," *Dissent,* Summer 1993, pp. 356–361.

Jacob, Margaret C., "Private Beliefs in Public Temples: The New Religiosity of the Eighteenth Century," *Social Research* 59, no. 1 (Spring 1992): 59–84.

Jamal, 'Abbashar, "Funding Fundamentalism: The Political Economy of an Islamist State," *Middle East Report,* no. 172 (September–October 1991).

Jansen, Willy, *Women Without Men: Gender and Marginality in an Algerian Town* (Leiden: E. J. Brill, 1987).

Johnson, James Turner, "Does Democracy 'Travel'? Some Thoughts on Democracy and Its Cultural Context," *Ethics and International Affairs* 6 (1992): 41–55.

Joseph, Suad, "Gender and Civil Society," *Middle East Report,* no. 183 (July–August, 1993), pp. 22–26.

Jowitt, Ken, "The New World Disorder," *Journal of Democracy* 2, no. 1 (Winter 1991): 11–20.

Juergensmeyer, Mark, *The New Cold War? Religious Nationalism Confronts the Secular State* (Berkeley: University of California Press, 1993).

Kadıoğlu, Ayşe, "Women's Subordination in Turkey: Is Islam Really the Villain?" *Middle East Journal* 48, no. 4 (Autumn 1994): 645–660.

Kamali, Mohammad H., "Freedom of Expression in Islam: An Analysis of Fitnah," *American Journal of Islamic Social Sciences* 10 (Summer 1993): 178–198.

——, "The Approved and Disapproved Varieties of Ra'y (Personal Opinion) in Islam," *The American Journal of Islamic Social Sciences* 7, no. 1 (March 1990): 39–65.

Kandiyoti, Deniz, "Women, Islam and the State," *Middle East Report,* no. 173 (November–December 1991).

——, "End of Empire: Islam, Nationalism and Women in Turkey," in *Women, Islam and the State,* Deniz Kandiyoti, ed. (London: Macmillan, 1991), pp. 22–47.

Karl, Terry Lynn, "Dilemmas of Democratization in Latin America," *Comparative Politics* 22 (October 1990): 1–21.

Katzman, Kenneth, *The Warriors of Islam: Iran's Revolutionary Guards* (Boulder, CO: Westview Press, 1993).

Kaufman, Edy, Shukri B. Abed, and Robert L. Rothstein, ed., *Democracy, Peace, and the Israeli-Palestinian Conflict* (Boulder, CO: Lynne Rienner Publishers, 1993).

Kazemi, Farhad, "Civil Society and Iranian Politics," in *Civil Society in the Middle East,* vol. 2, Augustus Richard Norton, ed. (Leiden, the Netherlands: E. J. Brill Publishers, 1995).

————, "Models of Iranian Politics, the Road to the Islamic Revolution, and the Challenge of Civil Society," *World Politics* 47 (forthcoming July 1995).

————, "The Military and Politics in Iran: The Uneasy Symbiosis," in *Iran: Toward Modernity—Studies in Thought, Politics, and Society,* Elie Kedourie and Sylvia Haim, eds. (London: Frank Cass, 1980).

Keane, John, *Civil Society and the State* (London: Verso Press, 1988).

————, ed., *Democracy and Civil Society: New European Perspectives* (London: Verso Press, 1988).

Kechichian, Joseph A., *Political Dynamics and Security in the Arabian Peninsula Through the 1990s* (Santa Monica, CA: Rand Corporation, 1993).

Keddie, Nikki, "Iranian Imbroglios: Who's Irrational?" *World Policy Journal* 5, no. 1 (Winter 1987–1988): 29–54.

Kedourie, Elie, *Democracy and Arab Political Culture* (Washington, DC: The Washington Institute for Near East Policy, 1992).

el-Kenz, Ali, *Algerian Reflections on the Arab Crisis* (Austin: Center for Middle Eastern Studies, University of Texas, 1991).

Kepel, Gilles, *Muslim Extremism in Egypt* (Berkeley: University of California Press, 1985).

Kerr, Malcolm, "Arab Radical Notions of Democracy," *St. Anthony's Papers,* no. 16 (1966).

Al-Khafaji, Isam, "Beyond the Ultra-Nationalist State," *Middle East Report,* nos. 187–188 (March–April/May–June 1994), pp. 34–39.

Khalaf, Issa, *Politics in Palestine, Arab Factionalism and Social Disintegration 1939–1948* (New York: State University of New York, 1991).

Khalaf, Samir, *Beirut Reclaimed: Reflections on Urban Design and the Restoration of Civility* (Beirut: Editions Dar al-Nahar, 1993).

al-Khalil, Samir, *The Republic of Fear* (Berkeley: University of California Press, 1989).

Khashan, Hilal, "The Quagmire of Arab Democracy," *Arab Studies Quarterly* 14, no. 1 (Winter 1992): 17–33.

————, "The Limits of Arab Democracy," *World Affairs* 153, no. 4 (Spring 1991): 127–135.

Khouri, Fred, *The Arab Israeli Dilemma* (Syracuse, NY: Syracuse University Press, 3d edition, 1985).

Khoury, Philip, "Syrian Urban Politics in Transition: The Quarters of Damascus During the French Mandate," *International Journal of Middle East Studies* 16, no. 4 (November 1984): 507–540.

Khuri, Fuad, *Tribe and State in Bahrain* (Chicago: University of Chicago Press, 1980).

Kienle, Eberhard, ed., *Contemporary Syria: Liberalization Between Cold War and Peace* (London: I. B. Tauris and Co., 1994).

Kimmerling, Baruch, *Zionism and Territory: The Socio-Territorial Dimensions of Zionist Politics* (Berkeley: Institute of International Studies, University of California, 1983).

Kirat, Mohamed, *The Communicators: A Portrait of Algerian Journalists and Their Work* (Algiers: Office des Publications Universitaires, 1993).

Knauss, Peter, *The Persistence of Patriarchy: Class, Gender, and Ideology in Twentieth Century Algeria* (New York: Praeger, 1987).

Korosenyi, Andras, "Stable or Fragile Democracy? Political Cleavages and Party System in Hungary," *Government and Opposition* 28 no. 1 (Winter 1993): 87–104.

Koury, Enver, *The United Arab Emirates: Its Political System and Politics* (Hyattsville, MD: Institute of Middle Eastern and North African Affairs, 1980).

Krämer, Gudrun, "Islamist Democracy," *Middle East Report,* no. 183 (July–August 1993), pp. 2–8.

———, "Liberalization and Democracy in the Arab World," *Middle East Report,* no. 174 (January–February 1992), pp. 22–25, 35.

Krasner, Stephen D., *Structural Conflict: The Third World Against Global Liberalism* (Berkeley: University of California Press, 1985).

Kretzmer, David, *The Legal Status of the Arabs in Israel* (Boulder, CO: Westview Press, 1990).

Lambton, Ann K. S., "Secret Societies and the Persian Revolution of 1905–6," *St. Antony's Papers* (London: Chatto and Windus, 1958).

Landau, Jacob M., "The National Salvation Party in Turkey," *Asian and African Studies* 11 (1976): pp. 1–57.

Lasch, Christopher, "Liberalism and Civic Virtue," *Telos,* no. 88 (Summer 1991).

Lawrence, Bruce, *Defenders of God: The Revolt Against the Modern Age* (San Francisco: Harper and Row, 1989).

Lawson, Fred, *Oppositional Movements and U.S. Policy Toward the Arab Gulf States,* "Critical Issues" series, no. 9 (New York: Council on Foreign Relations, 1992).

———, *Bahrain: The Modernization of Autocracy* (Boulder, CO: Westview Press, 1989).

———, "Class and State in Kuwait," *MERIP Reports,* no. 132 (May 1985), pp. 16–21, 32.

Lawson, Stephanie, "Conceptual Issues in the Comparative Study of Regime Change and Democratization," *Comparative Politics* 25, no. 2 (January 1993): 183–205.

Layachi, Azzadine, "Government, Legitimacy and Democracy in Algeria," *Maghreb Report* 1, no. 1 (January/February 1992): 3, 7.

Layachi, Azzedine, and Abdel-Kader Haireche, "National Development and Political Protest: Islamists in the Maghreb Countries," *Arab Studies Quarterly* 14, nos. 2–3 (Spring/Summer 1992): 69–92.

Leca, Jean, "Social Structure and Political Stability: Comparative Evidence from the Algerian, Syrian and Iraqi Cases," in *The Arab State,* Giacomo Luciani, ed. (Berkeley: University of California Press, 1990), pp. 150–188.

Lesch, Ann Mosely, "The Destruction of Civil Society in the Sudan," in *Civil Society in the Middle East,* vol. 2, Augustus Richard Norton, ed. (Leiden, the Netherlands: E. J. Brill Publishers, 1995).

———, "Negotiations in the Sudan," in *Foreign Intervention in Sub-Saharan Africa: Making War and Waging Peace,* David R. Smock, ed. (Washington, DC: U.S. Institute of Peace, 1993).

———, *Transition to Palestinian Self-Government: Practical Steps Toward Israeli-Palestinian Peace* (Cambridge, MA: American Academy of Arts and Sciences, 1992).

———, "Military Disengagement from Politics: The Sudan," in *Military Disengagement from Politics,* Constantine P. Danopoulos, ed. (New York: Routledge, 1988), pp. 26–29.

Liebman, Charles, and Eliezer Don-Yehiya, *Civil Religion in Israel* (Berkeley: University of California Press, 1983).

Levi-Faur, David, "Measuring the Strength of Civil Society in Israel: The (Business) Interest Groups Perspective," paper delivered at the Social Science History Association's Annual Meeting, Baltimore, MD, November 1993.

Lewis, Bernard, *The Shaping of the Modern Middle East* (New York: Oxford University Press, 1994).

————, "Islam and Liberal Democracy," *The Atlantic Monthly* 271, no. 2 (February 1993): 89–94.

————, *Islam and the West* (New York: Oxford University Press, 1993).

————, "Rethinking the Middle East," *Foreign Affairs* 17, no. 4 (Fall 1992).

————, "Democracy in the Middle East: Its State and Prospects," *Middle East Affairs* VI, no. 4 (April 1955): 101–108.

Lewis, Norman, "The Isma'ilis of Syria Today," *Journal of the Royal Central Asia Society* 39 (January 1952): 69–77.

Lewis, Peter M., "Political Transition and the Dilemma of Civil Society in Africa," *Journal of International Affairs* 42, no. 1 (Summer 1992): 31–54.

Lindenburg, Marc, and Shantayanan Devarajan, "Revisiting the Myths About Structural Adjustment, Democracy, and Economic Performance in Developing Countries," *Comparative Politics* 25, no. 2 (January 1993): 169–181.

Liphjart, Arend, *Democracies: Patterns of Majoritarian and Consensus Government in Twenty-One Countries* (New Haven, CT: Yale University Press, 1984).

Lippert, Anne, "Algerian Women's Access to Power: 1962–1985," in *Studies in Power and Class in Africa,* Irving Leonard Markovitz, ed. (New York: Oxford University Press, 1987), pp. 209–232.

Litani, Yehuda, "Leadership in the West Bank and Gaza," *Jerusalem Quarterly,* no. 14 (Winter 1980), pp. 90–109.

Locke, John, *Two Treatises of Government* [1968] (New York, NY: Cambridge University Press, 1988).

Lockman, Zachary, ed., *Workers and Working Classes in the Middle East: Struggle, Histories, Historiographies* (Albany, NY: SUNY Press, 1994).

Luciani, Giacomo, ed., *The Arab State* (Berkeley: University of California Press, 1990).

————, "Economic Foundations of Democracy and Authoritarianism: The Arab World in Comparative Perspective," *Arab Studies Quarterly* 10, no. 4 (1988).

Lustick, Ian, "Stability in Deeply Divided Societies: Consociationalism Versus Control," *World Politics* 31, no. 3 (1979): 321–349.

Maghraoui, Abdeslam, "Problems of Transition to Democracy: Algeria's Short-lived Experiment with Electoral Politics," *Middle East Insight* VIII, no. 6 (July–October 1992): 20–26.

Mahdavi, H., "The Pattern and Problems of Economic Development in Rentier States: The Case of Iran," in *Studies in the Economic History of the Middle East,* Michael Cook, ed. (London: Oxford University Press, 1970).

Maier, Charles, ed., *Changing Boundaries of the Political* (Cambridge: Cambridge University Press, 1987).

Makram-Ebeid, Mona, "Political Opposition in Egypt: Democratic Myth or Reality?" *Middle East Journal* 43, no. 3 (Summer 1989): 423–436.

Malwal, Bona, "The Agony of the Sudan," *Journal of Democracy* 1, no. 2 (Spring 1990): 75–86.

Mamdani, Mahmood, "Africa: Democratic Theory and Democratic Struggles— Clash Between Ideas and Realities?" *Dissent* (Summer 1992), pp. 312–318.

Mansfield, Peter, *A History of the Middle East* (Harmondsworth: Penguin, 1991).

Mardin, Şerif, "Civil Society: A Comparative Approach," unpublished paper, May 1993.

————, "The Nakşibendi Order in Turkish History," in *Islam in Modern Turkey: Religion, Politics and Literature in a Secular State,* Richard Tapper, ed. (London: I. B. Tauris, 1991), pp. 121–144.

————, *Religion and Social Change in Modern Turkey: The Case of Bediuzzaman Said Nursi* (Albany: State University of New York Press, 1989).

————, "Religion and Politics in Modern Turkey," in *Islam in the Political Process,* James P. Piscatori, ed. (London: Cambridge University Press, 1983), pp. 138–159.

————, "Center-Periphery Relations: A Key to Turkish Politics?" *Daedalus,* Winter 1973, pp. 169–190.

————, "Power, Civil Society, and Culture in the Ottoman Empire," *Comparative Studies in Society and History* 11 (June 1969): 258–281.

Marx, Karl, *The Marx-Engels Reader,* Robert Tucker, ed. (New York: W. W. Norton and Co., 1972).

Mayer, Ann E., *Islam and Human Rights: Tradition and Politics* (Boulder, CO: Westview Press, 1991).

McCormick, Basrett, Su Shaozhi, and Xiao Xiaoming, "The 1989 Democracy Movement: A Review of the Prospects for Civil Society in China," *Pacific Affairs* 65, no. 2 (Summer 1992): 182–202.

Meeker, Michael E., "The Muslim Intellectual and His Audience," in *Cultural Transitions in the Middle East,* Şerif Mardin, ed. (Leiden: E. J. Brill Publishers, 1994).

————, "The New Muslim Intellectuals in the Republic of Turkey," in *Islam in Modern Turkey: Religion, Politics and Literature in a Secular State,* Richard Tapper, ed. (London: I. B. Tauris, 1991), pp. 189–223.

Melucci, Alberto, "The Symbolic Challenge of Contemporary Movements," *Social Research* 52, no. 4 (Winter 1985): 789–816.

Merlin, Samuel, "Demography and Geography in Palestine," in *People and Politics in the Middle East,* Curtis Michael, ed. (New Brunswick, NJ: Transaction, 1971), pp. 182–204.

Mernissi, Fatima, *Islam and Democracy: Fear of the Modern World* (New York: Addison-Wesley, 1993).

Metral, Françoise, "State and Peasants in Syria: A Local View of a Government Irrigation Project," *Peasant Studies* 11, no. 2 (Winter 1984): 69–90.

Migdal, Joel S., "Civil Society in Israel," in *Rules and Rights in the Middle East: Democracy, Law and Society,* Ellis Goldberg, Resat Kasaba, and Joel Migdal, eds. (Seattle: University of Washington Press, 1993), pp. 119–138.

————, *Strong Societies and Weak States: State-Society Relations and State Capabilities in the Third World* (Princeton, NJ: Princeton University Press, 1988).

Migdal, Joel S., Atul Kohli, and Vivienne Shue, *State Power and Social Forces: Domination and Transformation in the Third World* (New York: Cambridge University Press, 1994).

Milani, Farzaneh, *Veils and Words: The Emerging Voices of Iranian Women Writers* (Syracuse, NY: Syracuse University Press, 1992).

Miller, Judith, "The Challenge of Radical Islam," *Foreign Affairs* 72, no. 2 (Spring 1993): 43–56.

Misztal, Bronislaw, and Barbara A. Misztal, "Democratization Processes as an Objective of New Social Movements," *Research in Social Movements, Conflicts and Change* 10 (1988): 93–106.

Mitchell, Richard, *The Society of Muslim Brothers* (London: Oxford University Press, 1964).

Mitchell, Timothy P., "The Limits of the State: Beyond Statist Approaches and Their Critics," *American Political Science Review* 85, no. 1 (March 1991): 77–96; follow-up comments by John Bendix, Bertell Ollman, and Bartholemew H. Sparrow, with a response by Timothy P. Mitchell, "Going Beyond the State?" *American Political Science Review* 86, no. 4 (December 1992): 1007–1021.

―――, "Everyday Methaphors of Power," *Theory and Society* 19 (1990): 545–577.

Mitchell, Timothy, and Roger Owen, "Defining the State in the Middle East," *Middle East Studies Association Bulletin* 24, no. 2 (December 1990): 179–183.

Moench, Richard U., "The May 1984 Elections in Egypt and the Question of Egypt's Stability," in *Elections in the Middle East: Implications of Recent Trends,* Linda L. Layne, ed. (Boulder, CO: Westview Press, 1987), pp. 47–85.

Mohamedi, Fareed, "Oman," in *The Persian Gulf States,* Helen Metz, ed. (Washington, DC: Library of Congress, 1995).

Moore, Barrington, *The Social Origins of Dictatorship and Democracy: Lord and Peasant in the Making of the Modern World* (Boston: Beacon Press, 1966).

Moore, Clement Henry, *Tunisia Since Independence: Dynamics of a One Party State* (Berkeley and Los Angeles: University of California Press, 1965).

Mortimer, Robert, "Algeria: The Clash Between Islam, Democracy and the Military," *Current History,* January 1993, pp. 37–41.

―――, "Islam and Multiparty Politics in Algeria," *Middle East Journal* 45, no. 4 (Autumn 1991): 575–593.

―――, "Global Economy and African Foreign Policy: The Algerian Model," *African Studies Review* 27, no. 1 (March 1984): 1–22.

―――, *The Third World Coalition in International Politics* (Boulder, CO: Westview Press, 1984).

―――, "The Algerian Revolution in Search of the African Revolution," *Journal of Modern African Studies* 8, no. 3 (October 1970): 363–387.

Moussalli, Ahmad, "Modern Islamic Fundamentalist Discourses on Civil Society, Pluralism, and Democracy," in *Civil Society in the Middle East,* vol. 1, Augustus Richard Norton, ed. (Leiden: E. J. Brill Publishers, 1994), pp. 79–119.

―――, *Radical Islamic Fundamentalism: The Ideological and Political Discourse of Sayyid Qutb* (Beirut: Amercian University of Beirut, 1992).

Munson, Henry, *Religion and Power in Morocco* (New Haven, CT: Yale University Press, 1993).

Muslih, Muhammad, "Palestinian Civil Society," in *Civil Society in the Middle East,* vol. 1, Augustus Richard Norton, ed. (Leiden: E. J. Brill Publishers, 1994), pp. 243–268.

―――, "The Golan: Israel, Syria, and Strategic Calculations," *Middle East Journal* 47, no. 4 (Autumn 1993): 611–632.

―――, "Palestinian Civil Society," *Middle East Journal* 47, no. 2 (Spring 1993): 258–274.

―――, *The Origins of Palestinian Nationalism* (New York: Columbia University Press and the Institute for Palestine Studies, 1988).

Muslih, Muhammad, and Augustus Richard Norton, "The Need for Arab Democracy," *Foreign Policy* 83 (Summer 1991): 3–19.

―――, *Political Tides in the Arab World* (New York: Foreign Policy Association, 1991).

al-Na'im, 'Abdullahi A., and Peter N. Kok, *Fundamentalism and Militarism: A Report on the Root Causes of Human Rights Violations in the Sudan* (New York: The Fund for Peace, February 1991).

Najmabadi, Afsaneh, "Hazards of Modernity and Morality: Women, State and Ideology in Contemporary Iran," in *Women, Islam and the State,* Deniz Kandiyot, ed. (Philadelphia, PA: Temple University, 1991), pp. 48–76.

Nakhleh, Khalil, *Indigenous Organizations in Palestine: Towards a Purposeful Societal Development* (Jerusalem: Arab Thought Forum, 1991).

al-Naqeeb, Khaldoun, *Society and State in the Gulf and Arab Peninsula: A Different Perspective* (London: Routledge, 1990).

Nashat, Guity, ed., *Women and Revolution in Iran* (Boulder, CO: Westview Press, 1983).

Nettl, J., "The State as a Conceptual Variable," *World Politics* 20 (1968): 559–592.

Niblock, Tim, and Emma Murphy, *Economic and Political Liberalization in the Middle East* (London: British Academic Press, 1993).

Noakes, Greg, "Islamism vs. the State in Algeria," *Middle East Affairs Journal* 1, no. 3 (Spring–Summer 1993): 14–28.

Nordlinger, Eric A., *On the Autonomy of the Democratic State* (Cambridge, MA: Harvard University Press, 1981).

Norton, Augustus Richard, ed., *Civil Society in the Middle East,* vols. 1 & 2 (Leiden: E. J. Brill Publishers, 1994 and 1995).

————, "The Future of Civil Society in the Middle East," *Middle East Journal* 47, no. 2 (Spring 1993): 205–216.

————, "Breaking Through the Wall of Fear in the Arab World," *Current History* 91, no. 561 (January 1992): 37–41.

————, "Toward Enduring Peace in the Middle East," in *The Struggle for Peace: Israelis and Palestinians,* Elizabeth Warnock Fernea and Mary Evelyn Hocking, eds. (Austin: University of Texas Press, 1992): 317–329.

Norton, Augustus Richard, and Jillian Schwedler, "Swiss Soldiers, Ta'if Clocks, and Early Elections: Toward a Happy Ending in Lebanon?" in *Peace for Lebanon? From War to Reconstruction,* Deirdre Collings, ed. (Boulder, CO: Lynne Rienner Publishers, 1994), pp. 45–65.

Nowshirvani, Vahid, and Patrick Clawson, "The State and Social Equity in Postrevolutionary Iran," in *The State and Social Transformations in Afghanistan, Iran, and Pakistan,* Myron Weiner and 'Ali Banuazizi, eds. (Syracuse, NY: Syracuse University Press, 1994), pp. 228–269.

Odhibat, Atef, "Civil Society in Jordan: A Preliminary Assessment," a paper presented at a conference in Giza, Egypt, 28–30 May 1992.

O'Donnell, Guillermo, *Modernization and Bureaucratic-Authoritarianism* (Berkeley: University of California Press, 1973).

O'Donnell, Guillermo, and Philippe C. Schmitter, *Transitions from Authoritarian Rule: Tentative Conclusions About Uncertain Democracies* (Baltimore, MD: Johns Hopkins University Press, 1986).

Offe, Claus, "New Social Movements: Challenging the Boundaries of Institutional Politics," *Social Research* 52, no. 4 (Winter 1985): 815–868.

Öncü, Ayse, "The Transformation of the Bases of Social Standing in Contemporary Turkish Society," in *Structural Change in Turkish Society,* Mübeccel Kiray, ed. (Bloomington, IN: Indiana University Turkish Studies 10, 1991), pp. 140–162.

Pateman, "The Fraternal Social Contract," in *Democracy and Civil Society: New European Perspectives,* John Keane, ed. (London: Verso Press, 1988).

Pelczynski, Z. A., ed., *The State and Civil Society: Studies in Hegel's Political Philosophy* (Cambridge: Cambridge University Press, 1984).

Peled, Yoav, "Ethnic Democracy and the Legal Construction of Citizenship: Arab Citizens of the Jewish State," *American Political Science Review* 86, no. 2 (1992): 432–443.

Peres, Yochanan, and Ephraim Yuchtman-Yaar, *Trends in Israeli Democracy: The Public's View* (Boulder, CO: Lynne Rienner Publishers, 1992).

Peretz, Don, *The Government and Politics of Israel* (Boulder, CO: Westview Press, 2d edition, 1983).

Perèz-Diàz, Victor M., *The Return of Civil Society: The Emergence of Democratic Spain* (Cambridge, MA: Harvard University Press, 1993).

Perry, Glenn E., "Democracy and Human Rights in the Shadow of the West," *Arab Studies Quarterly* 14, no. 4 (Fall 1992): 1–22.

Perthes, Volker, "A Look at Syria's Upper Class: The Bourgeoisie and the Ba'th," *Middle East Report*, no. 170 (May–June 1991): 31–37.

Peterson, J. E., *The Arab Gulf States: Steps Toward Political Participation* (New York: Praeger, 1988).

Pfeifer, Karen, *Agrarian Reform Under State Capitalism in Algeria* (Boulder, CO: Westview Press, 1985).

Piro, Timothy, "Parliament, Politics, and Pluralism in Jordan: Democratic Trends at a Difficult Time," *Middle East Insight* VIII, no. 6 (July–October 1992): 39–44.

Pripstein-Posusney, Marsha, "Irrational Workers: The Moral Economy of Labor Protest in Egypt," *World Politics* 46, no. 1 (October 1993): 83–120.

Przeworksi, Adam, *Democracy and the Market: Political and Economic Reforms in Eastern Europe and Latin America* (Cambridge: Cambridge University Press, 1991).

Putnam, Robert, *Making Democracy Work: Civic Traditions in Modern Italy* (Princeton: Princeton University Press, 1993).

Pye, Lucian W., "Political Science and the Crisis of Authoritarianism," *American Political Science Review* 84, no. 1 (March 1990): 3–19.

Quandt, William B., Fuad Jabber, and Ann M. Lesch, *The Politics of Palestinian Nationalism* (Los Angeles: University of California Press, 1977).

Rabushka, Alvin, *A Theory of Racial Harmony* (Columbia, SC: South Carolina Press, 1974).

Rahnema, 'Ali, and Farhad Nomani, *The Secular Miracle: Religion, Politics and Economic Policy in Iran* (London: Zed, 1990).

Rahnema, Saeed, "Work Councils in Iran: The Illusion of Worker Control," *Economic and Industrial Democracy* 13 (February 1992): 81–85.

Rajaee, Farhang, *Islamic Values and World View: Khomeyni on Man, the State, and International Politics* (Lanham, MD: University Press of America, 1983).

Ramazani, Nesta, "Women in Iran: The Revolutionary Ebb and Flow," *Middle East Journal* 47, no. 3 (Summer 1993): 409–428.

———, "Islamic Fundamentalism and the Women of Kuwait," *Middle East Insight* (January/February 1988).

Rau, Zbigniew, *The Reemergence of Civil Society in Eastern Europe and the Soviet Union* (Boulder, CO: Westview Press, 1991).

Razi, G. Hossein, "Legitimacy, Religion, and Nationalism in the Middle East," *American Political Science Review* 84, no. 1 (March 1990): 69–91.

Richards, Alan, "Economic Pressures for Accountable Governance in the Middle East and North Africa," in *Civil Society in the Middle East*, vol. 1, Augustus Richard Norton, ed. (Leiden: E. J. Brill Publishers, 1994), pp. 55–78.

———, "Economic Imperatives and Political Systems," *Middle East Journal* 47, no. 2 (Spring 1993): 217–227.

Richards, Alan, and John Waterbury, *A Political Economy of the Middle East* (Boulder, CO: Westview Press, 1990).

Riker, H. William, *The Theory of Political Coalitions* (New Haven, CT: Yale University Press, 1962).

Roberts, John, "Prospects for Democracy in Jordan," *Arab Studies Quarterly* 13, nos. 3 and 4 (Summer/Fall 1991): 119–138.

Robinson, Glenn E., "The Role of the Professional Middle Class in the Mobilization of Palestinian Society: The Medical and Agricultural Committees," *International Journal of Middle East Studies* 25, no. 2 (May 1993): 301–326.

Rochon, Thomas R., "Political Change in Ordered Societies: The Rise of Citizens' Movements," *Comparative Politics* (April 1983).

Rosefsky-Wickham, Carrie, "Beyond Democratization: Political Change in the Arab World," *PS: Political Science & Politics,* September 1994, pp. 507–509.

Rostovzeff, Michael Ivanovitch, *Caravan Cities* (Oxford: The Clarendon Press, 1932).

Roy, Olivier, *The Failure of Political Islam,* Carol Volk, trans. [from French] (Cambridge: Harvard University Press, 1994).

Roy, Sara, "Civil Society in the Gaza Strip," in *Civil Society in the Middle East,* vol. 2, Augustus Richard Norton, ed. (Leiden, the Netherlands: E. J. Brill Publishers, 1995).

———, "The Seed of Chaos, and of Night: The Gaza Strip After the Agreement," *Journal of Palestine Studies* 23, no. 4 (Spring 1994).

———, "Gaza: New Dynamics of Civic Disintegration," *Journal of Palestine Studies* 22, no. 4 (Summer 1993): 24–26.

Rueschemeyer, Dietrich, Evelyne Huber Stephens, and John D. Stephens, *Capitalist Development and Democracy* (Chicago: University of Chicago Press, 1992).

Rugh, William, *The Arab Press* (Syracuse, NY: Syracuse University Press, 1987).

Rustow, Dankwart, "Transitions to Democracy," *Comparative Politics* 2, no. 3 (1970): 337–363.

Sadowski, Yahya, "The New Orientalism and the Democracy Debate," *Middle East Report,* no. 183 (July–August 1993): 14–21, 40.

Salamé, Ghassan, "Islam and the West," *Foreign Policy* 90 (Spring 1993): 22–37.

———, "Political Power and the Saudi State," *MERIP Reports,* no. 91 (October 1980).

Sales, Arnaud, "The Private, the Public, and Civil Society: Social Realms and Power Structures," *International Political Science Review* 12, no. 4 (1991): 295–312.

Sanasarian, Eliz, "Political Activism and Islamic Identity in Iran," in *Women in the World, 1975–1985: The Women's Decade,* Lynne Igitzin and Ruth Ross, eds. (Santa Barbara, CA: ABC Clio Press, 1986).

———, *The Women's Rights Movement in Iran* (New York: Praeger, 1982).

Sarabi, Farzin, "The Post-Khomeini Era in Iran: The Elections to the Fourth Islamic Majlis," *Middle East Journal* 48 (Winter 1994): 89–107.

Saracoglu, Rügdü, "Liberalization of the Economy," *Politics in the Third Turkish Republic,* Metin Heper and A. Evin, eds. (Boulder, CO: Westview Press, 1994), pp. 63–76.

Sayari, Sabri, ed., *Democratization in the Middle East: Trends and Prospects* (Washington, DC: National Academy Press, 1993).

———, "Political Patronage in Turkey," in *Patrons and Clients in Mediterranean Societies,* Ernest Gellner and John Waterbury, eds. (London: Dockworth's Press, 1977).

al-Sayyid, Mustapha K., "A Civil Society in Egypt?" in *Civil Society in the Middle East,* vol. 1, Augustus Richard Norton, ed. (Leiden: E. J. Brill Publishers, 1994), pp. 269–293.

———, "A Civil Society in Egypt?" *Middle East Journal* 47, no. 2 (Spring 1993): 228–242.

———, "Slow Thaw in the Arab World," *World Policy Journal* 8, no. 4 (Fall 1991): 711–738.

Schmitter, Philippe C., and Terry Lynn Karl, "What Democracy Is and Is Not," *Journal of Democracy* 2, no. 3 (Summer 1991).

Schwedler, Jillian, "Early Elections in the West Bank and Gaza," *Middle East Insight* VIII, no. 6 (July–October 1992): 5–9.

Segal, Zeev, *Israeli Democracy: Constitutional Principles in the Government of the State of Israel* (Tel Aviv: Department of Defence Publishing House, 1988).

Seligman, Adam, *The Idea of Civil Society* (New York: The Free Press, 1992).

———, "Trust and the Meaning of Civil Society," *International Journal of Politics, Culture and Society* 6, no. 1 (1992): 5–21.

Serberny-Mohammadi, Annabelle, and 'Ali Mohammadi, "Hegemony and Resistance: Media Politics in the Islamic Republic of Iran," *Quarterly Review of Film and Video* 12 (1991).

Sfeir, George N., "Source of Law and the Issue of Legitimacy and Rights," *Middle East Journal* 42, no. 3 (Summer 1988): 436–446.

Shaaban, Bouthaina, *Both Right and Left Handed: Arab Women Talk About Their Lives* (Bloomington: Indiana University Press, 1988).

Shaari, Yehuda, *Toward Social Liberalism* (Tel Aviv: Forder's Liberal School Publication, 1992).

Shalev, Michael, "Jewish Organized Labor and the Palestinians: A Study of State/Society Relations in Israel," in *The Israeli State and Society,* Kimmerling Baruch, ed. (Albany: State University of New York Press, 1989), pp. 93–133.

Shambayati, Hootan, "The Rentier State, Interest Groups, and the Paradox of Autonomy: State and Business in Turkey and Iran," *Comparative Politics* 26, no. 3 (April 1994): 307–331.

Sharabi, Hisham, ed., *The Next Arab Decade: Alternative Futures* (Boulder, CO: Westview Press, 1988).

———, *Neopatriarchy: A Theory of Distorted Change in Arab Society* (Oxford: Oxford University Press, 1988).

Shehadeh, Raja, "Questions of Jurisdiction: A Legal Analysis of the Gaza-Jericho Agreement," *Journal of Palestine Studies* 23, no. 4 (Summer 1994).

———, "Negotiating Self-Government Arrangements," *Journal of Palestine Studies* 21, no. 84 (Summer 1992): 22–32.

Sheikholeslami, Reza, "The Patrimonial Structure of Iranian Bureaucracy in the Late Nineteenth Century," *Iranian Studies,* 11 (1978).

Shils, Edward. "The Virtue of Civil Society," *Government and Opposition* 26, no. 1 (Winter 1992): 3–20.

———, *Center and Periphery: Essays in Macrosociology* (Chicago: University of Chicago Press, 1975).

Shubane, Khela, "The Unfinished Revolution: Civil Society in South Africa," *Journal of Democracy* 2, no. 3 (Summer 1991): 53–55.

Siavoshi, Sussan, "Factionalism and Iranian Politics: The Post-Khomeini Experience," *Iranian Studies* 25 (1992): 27–49.

Simon, Roger, "Civil Society, the State, and the Nature of Power," *Gramsci's Political Thought: An Introduction* (London: Lawrence & Wishart, 1982).

Singerman, Diane, *Avenues of Participation: Family, Politics, and Networks in Urban Quarters of Cairo* (Princeton, NJ: Princeton University Press, 1995).

Sirowy, Larry, and Alex Inkeles, "Effects of Democracy on Economic Growth and Inequality: A Review," *Studies in Comparative International Development* 25, no. 1 (Spring 1990): 126–157.

Sivan, Emmanuel, *Radical Islam* (New Haven, CT: Yale University Press, 1985).

Skoçpol, Theda, "Bringing the State Back In," in *Comparative Politics: Notes and Readings,* Roy C. Macridis and Bernard E. Brown, eds. (Pacific Grove, CA: Brooks/Cole, 1990), pp. 58–67.

Slyomovics, Susan, "Cartoon Commentary: Algerian and Moroccan Caricatures from the Gulf War," *Middle East Report* 23, no. 1 (January–February 1993): 21–24.

Solinger, Dorothy J., "China's Transients and the State: A Form of Civil Society?" *Politics & Society* 21, no. 1 (March 1993): 91–122.

Springborg, Patricia, *Western Republicanism and the Oriental Prince* (Austin: University of Texas Press, 1992).

Springborg, Robert, "State-Society Relations in Egypt: The Debate over Owner-Tenant Relations," *Middle East Journal* 45, no. 2 (Spring 1991): 232–249.

———, *Mubarak's Egypt: Fragmentation of the Political Order* (Boulder, CO: Westview Press, 1989).

Sprinzak, Ehud, and Larry Diamond, *Israeli Democracy Under Stress* (Boulder, CO: Lynne Rienner Publishers, 1993).

Stephan, Alfred, "The Tasks of a Democratic Opposition," *Journal of Democracy* 1, no. 2 (Spring 1990): 41–49.

Suleiman, Michael W., "Elections in a Confessional Democracy," *Journal of Politics* 29, no. 1 (February 1967): 109–128.

Sullivan, Denis J., *Private Voluntary Organizations in Egypt: Islamic Development, Private Initiative, and State Control* (Gainesville: University Press of Florida, 1994).

Sunar, Ilkay, "Populism and Patronage: The Demokrat Party and Its Legacy in Turkey," *Il Politico,* October–December 1990, pp. 745–757.

Sunar, Ilkay, and Binnaz Toprak, "Islam in Politics: The Case of Turkey," *Government and Opposition* 18 (1983): 421–441.

Tamari, Salim, "Left in Limbo: Leninist Heritage and Islamist Challenge," *Middle East Report,* no. 179 (November/December 1992), pp. 16–22.

Tamimi, Azzaz, ed., *Power-Sharing Islam?* (London: Liberty for Muslim World Publications, 1993).

Taraki, Lisa, "Mass Organizations in the West Bank," in *Occupation: Israel Over Palestine,* 2d edition, Naseer H. Aruri, ed. (Belmont, MA: Association of Arab-American University Graduates, 1989), pp. 431–463.

Tarkowska, Elzbieta, and Jacek Tarkowski, "Social Disintegration in Poland: Civil Society or Amoral Familism?" *Telos,* no. 89 (Fall 1991), p. 108.

Taylor, Charles, "Modes of Civil Society," *Public Culture* 3, no. 1 (Fall 1990): 95–132.

Tétreault, Mary Ann, "Civil Society in Kuwait: Protected Spaces and Women's Rights," *Middle East Journal* 47, no. 2 (Spring 1993): 275–291.

Tibi, Bassam, "Islam and Arab Nationalism," in *The Islamic Impulse,* Barbara Freyer Stowasser, ed. (Washington, DC: Center for Contemporary Arab Studies, 1987), pp. 59–74.

———, "The Renewed Role of Islam in the Political and Social Development of the Middle East," *Middle East Journal* 37, no. 1 (Winter 1983): 3–13.

Tilly, Charles, "Models and Realities of Popular Collective Action," *Social Research* 52, no. 4 (Winter 1985): 717–747.

Tlemcani, Rachid, "The Rise of Algerian Women: Cultural Dualism and Multi-Party Politics," *Journal of Developing Societies* VIII (1993): 69–81.

———, "Chadli's Perestroika," *Middle East Report,* no. 163 (March–April 1990), pp. 14–17.

de Tocqueville, Alexis, *Democracy in America*, vols. 1 and 2 (New York: Langley Press, 1845).

Toprak, Binnaz, "Civil Society in Turkey," in *Civil Society in the Middle East*, vol. 2, Augustus Richard Norton, ed. (Leiden, the Netherlands: E. J. Brill Publishers, 1995).

————, "Women and Fundamentalism: The Case of Turkey," in *Identity Politics and Women*, Valentine M. Mogdaham, ed. (Boulder, CO: Westview Press, 1994), pp. 293–306.

————, "Islamist Intellectuals: Revolt Against Industry and Technology," in *Turkey and the West: Changing Political and Cultural Identities*, Metin Heper, Ayse Öncü, and Heinz Kramer, eds. (London: I. B. Tauris, 1993), pp. 237–257.

————, "Religion as State Ideology in a Secular Setting: The Turkish-Islamic Synthesis," in *Aspects of Religion in Secular Turkey*, Occasional Paper Series, no. 40, Malcolm Wagstaff, ed. (Durham: University of Durham, Centre for Middle Eastern and Islamic Studies, 1990), pp. 10–16.

————, "Islamist Intellectuals of the 1980s in Turkey," *Current Turkish Thought* 62 (1987).

Touraine, Alain, "An Introduction to the Study of Social Movements," *Social Research* 52, no. 4 (Winter 1985): 749–787.

————, "Triumph or Downfall of Civil Society," David Rieff et al., ed., *Humanities in Review*, vol. 1 (London: Cambridge University Press, 1982), pp. 218–234.

al-Turabi, Hasan, "Islam, Democracy, the State and the West: Summary of a Lecture and Roundtable Discussion with Hasan al-Turabi," prepared by Louis Cantouri and Arthur Lowrie, *Middle East Policy* 1, no. 3 (1992): 52–54.

Turner, Brian S., "Orientalism and the Problem of Civil Society in Islam," in *Orientalism, Islam and Islamicists*, Asaf Hussain, Robert Olson, and Jamil Quereishi, eds. (Brattleboro, VT: Amana Books, 1984), pp. 23–42.

Vitalis, Robert, "The Democratization Industry and the Limits of the New Interventionism," *Middle East Report*, nos. 187–188 (March–April/May–June 1994), pp. 46–50.

von Sivers, Peter, "Retreating States and Expanding Societies: The State Autonomy/ Informal Civil Society Dialectic in the Middle East and North Africa," unpublished paper of the Joint Committee on the Near and Middle East and North Africa, Research Agenda, Social Science Research Council, 1986–1987.

Waltz, Susan E., "Making Waves: The Political Impact of Human Rights Groups in North Africa," *The Journal of Modern African Studies* 29, no. 3 (1991): 481–504.

————, "Another View of Feminine Networks: Tunisian Women and the Development of Political Efficacy," *International Journal of Middle East Studies* 22, no. 1 (February 1990): 21–36.

Walzer, Michael, "The Civil Society Argument," in *Dimensions of Radical Democracy: Pluralism, Citizenship, Community*, Chantal Mouffe, ed. (London: Verso, 1992), pp. 89–107.

————, "The Idea of Civil Society," *Dissent*, Spring 1991, pp. 293–304.

————, "The Civil Society Argument: the Good Life," *New Statesman & Society* 2 (October 6, 1989): 28–31.

Waterbury, John, "Democracy Without Democrats? The Potential for Political Liberalization in the Middle East," in *Democracy Without Democrats?* Ghassan Salamé, ed. (London: I. B. Taurus, 1994).

Wedeman, Ben, "Democracy in Jordan: Election Results Send Mixed Signals of Peace Process," *Middle East Insight* X, no. 1 (November–December 1993): 9–13.

Weigle, Marcia A., and Jim Butterfield, "Civil Society in Reforming Communist Regimes: The Logic of Emergence," *Comparative Politics* 25, no. 1 (October 1992): 1–24.

Weiner, Richard R., "Retrieving Civil Society in a Postmodern Epoch," *The Social Science Journal* 28, no. 3 (1991): 307–323.

White, Jenny B., *Money Makes Us Relatives: Women's Labor in Urban Turkey* (Austin: University of Texas Press, 1994).

Wittfogel, Karl, *Oriental Despotism* (New Haven, CT: Yale University Press, 1957).

Wood, Ellen Meiksins, "The Uses and Abuses of Civil Society," in *Socialist Register,* Ralph Miliband, ed., (Atlantic Highlands, NJ: Humanities Press, 1990), pp. 60–84.

Woods, Dwayne, "Civil Society in Europe and Africa: Limiting State Power Through a Public Sphere," *African Studies Review* 35, no. 2 (September 1992): 77–100.

Yishai, Yael, *Interest Groups in Israel: The Test of Democracy* (Tel Aviv: Am Oved, 1987).

Yongo-Bure, Benaiah, "Sudan's Deepening Crisis," *Middle East Report,* no. 172 (September–October 1991).

Zonis, Marvin, *The Political Elite of Iran* (Princeton, NJ: Princeton University Press, 1971).

Zoubir, Yahia, "The Painful Transition from Authoritarianism in Algeria," *Arab Studies Quarterly* 15, no. 3 (Summer 1993): 83–110.

Zubaida, Sami, *Islam, The People and the State: Political Ideas and Movements in the Middle East* (London: I. B. Tauris and Co., 1994).

———, "Islam, the State, and Democracy: Contrasting Conceptions of Society in Egypt," *Middle East Report,* no. 179 (November–December 1992), pp. 2–10.

Zureik, Elia, "Theoretical Considerations for a Sociological Study of the Arab State," *Arab Studies Quarterly* 3, no. 3 (Summer 1981): 229–257.

French–Language Sources

Aarts, Paul, "Les limites du "tribalisme politique": le Koweit d'après-guerre et le processus de démocratisation," *Monde arabe Maghreb—Machrek,* no. 142 (October–December 1993), pp. 61–79.

Addi, Lahouari, "Vers quel Contrat Social?" *Les Cahiers de l'Orient,* no. 23 (1991), pp. 21–28.

———, *État et Pouvoir* (Algiers: OPU, 1990).

———, *Impasse du Populisme* (Algiers: ENAL, 1990).

———, "Dynamique et contradictions du système politique algérien," *Revue Algérienne des Sciences Juridiques, Economiques et Politiques* 26 (June 1988): 495–508.

Ahano, M., "L'Etat en Iran," *Cahiers D'Etudes sur la Mediterranee Orientale et le Monde Turco-Iranian* 5 (1988): 23–51.

al-Ahnaf, Mustafa, Bernard Botiveau, and Frank Frégosi, *L'Algérie par les Islamistes* (Paris: Karthala, 1991).

Aïnad-Tabet, Nadia, "Participation des algériennes à la vie du pays," in *Femmes et politique autour de la méditerranée* (Paris: L'Harmattan, 1980), pp. 235–250.

el-Aoufi, Noureddine, ed., *La Société Civile au Maroc: Approches* (Rabat: Société Marocaine des Editeurs Réunis, 1992).

Badie, Bertrand, *Les Deux Etats: Pouvoir et Société en Occident et en Terre d'Islam* (Paris: Fayard, 1986).

Bekkar, Rabia, "Territoires des Femmes à Tlemcen: Pratiques et Représentations," *Monde Arabe: Maghreb-Machrek,* no. 143 (January–March 1994), pp. 126–141.

Belbah, Mustapha, "A la Recherche des 'Musulmans de France,'" in *Exiles et Royaumes: Les Appartenances au Monde Arabo-Musulman Aujourd'hui,* Gilles Kepel, ed. (Paris: Presses de la FNSP, 1994), pp. 331–345.

Bennoune, Mahfoud, and Ali El-Kenz, *Le hasard et l'histoire: entretiens avec Belaid Abdesselam,* vols. 1 & 2 (Algiers: ENAG/Editions, 1990).

Bentaleb, Fatima, "La rente dans la société et la culture en Algérie," *Peuples Méditerranéens* 26 (January–March 1984): 75–104.

Benzerfa-Guerroudj, Zineb, "Les Associations Feminines en Algérie," *Journal of Maghrebi Studies* 1–2, no. 1 (Spring 1991): 17–26.

Brahimi, Brahim, *Le Pouvoir, la Presse et les Intellectuels en Algérie* (Paris: L'Harmattan, 1989).

Bucaille, Laetitia, "L'Engagement islamiste des femmes en Algérie," *Monde Arabe: Maghreb-Machrek* 144 (April–June 1994): 105–118.

Burgat, François, "La mobilisation islamiste et les élections Algériennes du 12 juin 1990," *Maghreb-Machrek* 129 (July–September 1990): 5–22.

———, *L'Islamisme au Maghreb: La Voix du Sud* (Paris: Editions Karthala, 1988).

Cesari, Jocelyne, "Algérie: Contexte et Acteurs du Combat pour les Droits de l'Homme," *Monde Arabe: Maghreb-Machrek,* no. 142 (October–December 1993), pp. 24–31.

Chidiac, Louise-Marie, Abdo Kahi, and Antoine Messarra, eds., *La Generation de la Releve: La Pedagogie du Civisme* (Beirut: Bureau Pedagogique des Saints-Coeurs, 1992).

Cornand, Jocelyne, "L'Artisanat du Textile a Alep survie au Dynamisme?" *Bulletin d'Etudes Orientales Institut Français de Damas* XXXVI (1984).

Delaunoy, Geneviève, "La Press Algérienne et les Fantômes de la Liberté," *Le Monde Diplomatique* (May 1992), p. 12.

Destanne de Bernis, Gérard, "Les industries industrialisantes et les options Algériennes," *Tiers-Monde* 12 (1971): 545–563.

el-Difraoui, 'Abdelasiem, "La Critique du Système Démocratique par le Front Islamique du Salut," in *Exils et Royaumes: Les Appartenances Arabo-Musulman Aujourd'hui,* Gilles Kepel, ed. (Paris: Presses de la Fondation Nationale des Sciences Politiques, 1994), pp. 105–124.

Djeghloul, Abdelkader, "Le multipartisme à l'Algérienne," *Maghreb-Machrek* 127 (January–March 1990): 194–210.

Ecrement, Marc, *Indépendence politique et libération économique: Un quart de siècle du développement de l'Algérie: 1965–1985* (Algiers: ENAP-OPU; Grenoble: Presses Universitaires de Grenoble, 1986).

Fontaine, Jacques, "Les Elections Législatives Algériennes: Résultats du Premier Tour—26 Décembre 1991," *Monde Arabe: Maghreb-Machrek,* no. 135 (January–March 1992), pp. 155–165.

Fontaine, Jacques, "Les Élections Locales Algériennes du 12 juin 1990: Approche statistique et géographique," *Maghreb-Machrek* 129 (July-August-September 1990): 124–140.

Garon, Lisa, "La Presse et la Transition Democratique dans les Sociétés Arabes: Le Cas de l'Algérie," unpublished paper.

Gellner, Ernest, and Jean-Claude Vatin, eds., *Islam et politique au Maghreb* (Aix-en-Provence: CRESM, 1981).

Göle, Nilüfer, *Musulmanes ets modernes: voile et civilisation en turquiee* (Paris: Éditions la Découverte, 1993).

———, "Femmes voilées en Egypte et en Turquie," *Dossiers du Cedej* (Cairo, 1992), pp. 143–152.

———, "Ingénieurs musulmans et étudiantes voilées en Turquie," in *Intellectuels et militants de l'Islam contemporain,* Gilles Kepel and Y. Richards, eds. (Paris: le Seuil, 1990), pp. 167–191.

Grimaud, Nicole, "Prolongements Externes des Elections Algériennes," *Les Cahiers del'Orient,* no. 23 (1991), pp. 29–40.

———, *La Politique extérieure de l'Algérie* (Paris: Karthala, 1984).

———, "Nouvelles orientations de relations entre la France et l'Algérie," *Maghreb-Machrek,* no. 103 (January–March 1984), pp. 96–106.

Hadj 'Ali, Smaïl, "L'Islamisme dans la Ville: Espace Urbain et Contre-Centralité," *Monde Arabe: Maghreb-Machrek,* no. 143 (January–March 1994), pp. 69–74.

Hakiki-Talahite, Fatiha, "Sous le Voile . . . Les Femmes," *Les Cahiers de l'Orient* 23 (1991): 123–142.

Hermassi, Mohamed Abdelbeki, "L'Etat Tunisien et le Mouvement Islamiste," *Annuaire de l'Afrique du Nord* 28 (1989): 297–308.

———, "La Societé Tunisienne au Miroir Islamiste," *Maghreb-Machrek,* no. 103 (1984), pp. 39–56.

Kapil, Arun, "Chiffres-Clés Pour une Analyse: Portrait Statistiques des Elections du 12 Juin 1990," *Les Cahiers de l'Orient,* no. 23 (1991), pp. 41–63.

———, "Les Partis Islamistes en Algérie: Eléments de Présentation," *Monde Arabe: Maghreb-Machrek,* no. 133 (July–September 1991), pp. 103–111.

el-Kenz, 'Ali, *Au fil de la crise: Quatre études sur l'Algérie et le monde Arabe* (Algiers: Bouchène, 1989).

Kepel, Gilles and Yann Richard, eds., *Intellectuals et Militants de l'Islam Contemporain* (Paris: Seuil, 1990).

Kodmani-Darwish, Bassma, ed., *Maghreb: Les années de transition* (Paris: Masson, 1990).

Laacher, Smain, *Algérie: Réalités sociales et pouvoir* (Paris: L'Harmattan, 1985).

Labat, Séverine, "Islamismes et Islamistes en Algérie: Un Nouveau Militantisme," in *Exils et Royaumes: Les Appartenances au Monde Arabo-Musulman Aujourd'hui,* Gilles Kepel, ed. (Paris: Presses de la Fondation Nationale des Sciences Politiques, 1994), pp. 41–67.

Leca, Jean, "Etat et société en Algérie," in *Maghreb: Les années de transition,* Bassma Kodmani-Darwish, ed. (Paris: Masson, 1990), pp. 17–58.

Leca, Jean, and Nicole Grimaud, "L'Algérie face au contre-choc pétrolier," *Maghreb-Machrek* 112 (April–June 1986): 94–101.

———, "Le secteur privé en Algérie," *Maghreb-Machrek* 113 (July–September 1986): 102–119.

Lemoine, Maurice, "L'Algérie au risque des impatiences," *Le Monde Diplomatique* 48 (July 1991): 1, 12–13.

Leveau, Rémy, *Le sabre et le turban: L'avenir du Maghreb* (Paris: François Bourin, 1993).

Liabes, Djillali, "La Démocratie en Algérie: Culture et Contre-Culture," *Peuples Méditerranéens,* nos. 52–53 (July–December 1990), pp. 47–56.

Martinez, Luis, "Les Eucalyptus, Banlieu d'Alger, dans la Guerre Civile: Les Facteurs de la Mobilisation Islamiste," in *Exils et Royaumes: Les Appartenances Arabo-Musulmane Aujourd'hui,* Gilles Kepel, ed. (Paris: Presses de la Fondation Nationale des Sciences Politiques, 1994), pp. 89–104.

Marzouk, Mohsen, "Autonomie des Associations Tunisiennes: Les Enjeux Politiques," *L'Observateur,* no. 28, 8 October 1993, pp. 25–27.

Picard, Elizabeth, "Ouverture economique et renforcement militaire en Syrie," *Oriente Moderno,* Anno LIX (Luglio–Dicembre 1979).

Raffinot, Marc, and Pierre Jacquemot, *Le capitalisme d'état Algérien* (Paris: Maspero, 1977).

Redjala, Ramdane, *L'opposition en Algérie depuis 1962,* vol. 1 (Paris: L'Harmattan, 1988).

Rouadjia, Ahmed, *Les Frères et la Mosquée: Enquête sur le Mouvement Islamiste en Algérie* (Paris: Karthala, 1990).

———, "Doctrine et Discours du Cheikh Abbassi," *Peuples Méditerranéens,* nos. 52–53 (July–December 1990), pp. 167–180.

Salamé, Ghassan, "Sur la Causalite d'un Manque: Pourquoi le monde arabe n'est-il donc pas democratique?" *Revue Francaise Science Politique* 41, no. 3 (Juin 1991).

Sanson, Henri, *La cité Islamique en Algérie* (Paris: CNRS, 1983).

Shayegan, Daryush, *Le regard mutilé* (Paris: Albin Michel, 1989).

Taarji, Hinde, *Les Voilées de l'Islam,* 2d ed. (Casablanca: Editions Eddif, 1991).

Terrel, Hervé [pseud.], "L'Enclave Islamique de la Rue Jean-Pierre-Timbaud," in *Exils et Royaumes: Les Appartenances au Monde Arabo-Musulman Aujourd'hui,* Gilles Kepel, ed. (Paris: Presses de la FNSP, 1994), pp. 347–363.

Vergès, Meriem, "La Casbah d'Alger: Chronique de Survie dans un Quartier en Sursis," in *Exils et Royaumes: Les Appartenances Arabo-Musulman Aujourd'hui,* Gilles Kepel, ed. (Paris: Presses de la Fondation Nationale des Sciences Politiques, 1994), pp. 69–88.

Waterbury, John, "Une démocratie sans démocrates?" in *Démocraties sans démocrates, Politiques d'ouverture dans le monde arabe et Islamique,* Ghassan Salamé, ed. (Paris: Fayard, 1994), pp. 111–115.

Yefsah, Abdelkader, *La question du pouvoir en Algérie* (Algiers: ENAP, 1990).

Zartman, I. William, "L'élite algérienne sous la présidence de Chadli Benjedid," *Maghreb-Machrek,* no. 106 (October–November 1984), pp. 37–53.

Zghal, Abdelkadir, "Le Concept de Societé Civile et la Transition vers Le Multipartisme," *Annuaire de l'Afrique du Nord* 28 (1989): 207–228.

Zghidi, Salah, "A Question Democratique au Maghreb: Equivoques et Incomprehensions" *Esprit,* 1992.

Turkish-Language Sources

Bulaç, 'Ali, "Islam'i ve Tarihini Okuma Biçimi: Anthropolojik ve Modernist Yaklaşimin Eleştirisi," *Bilgi ve Hikmet,* no. 7 (Summer 1994).

Çakir, Ruşen, *Ne Şeriat Ne Demokrasi: Refah Partisini Anlamak* [Neither Shari'ah Nor Democracy] (Istanbul: Metis Yayinlari, 1994).

Gülmez, Mesut, "Insan Haklarinda Gelişmeler: ILO Sözleşmesinin Onaylanması," *Insan Hakları Yıllığı* 14 (1992): 177–196.

Güzel, Hasan Celal, "Ekonomik ve Sosyal Etüdler Konferans Heyeti," in *Sivil Topluma Geçi* (Istanbul: Acar Matbaacılık, 1992), pp. 31–44.

Kilinç, Ismail, "Türkiye'de Kentlesmenin Özellikleri," *Amme Idaresi Dergisi,* June 1993.

Mardin, Şerif, *Din ve Ideoloji* (Ankara, Siyasal Bilgiler Fakültesi, 1969).

Parla, Taha, *Türkiye'nin Siyasal Rejimi, 1980–1989* (Istanbul: Iletişim Yayınları, 1993).

———, *Türkiye'de Anayasalar* (Istanbul: Iletişim Yayınları, 1991).

Saribay, 'Ali Yaar, *Türkiye'de Modernle me, Din ve Parti Politikasi: MSP Örnek Olayi* (Istanbul: Alan Yayincilik, 1985).

Tarhanli, Iştar B., *Müslüman Toplum, "Laik" Devlet: Türkiye'de Diyanet Işleri Başkanliği* (Istanbul: Afa Yayinlari, 1993).

Toprak, Zafer, "Tanzimat ve Çağdaş Türkiye," *Toplum ve Bilim,* Summer–Fall 1989, pp. 41–55.

———, *Türkiye'de "Milli Iktisat" (1908–1918)* (Istanbul: Yurt Yayinlari, 1982).

———, "Halkçilik Ideolojisinin Oluşumu," Iktisadi ve Ticari Bilimler Akademisi Mezunlari Derneği, *Atatürk Döneminin Ekonomik ve Toplumsal Sorunlari* (Istanbul, Murat Matbaacilik, 1977), pp. 13–31.

Toroslu, Nevzat, "Ceza Muhakemesinde Yapılan Son Değişiklikler," *Insan Hakları Yılliği* 14 (1992): 13–24.

Tunaya, Tarik Zafer, *Türkiye'de Siyasal Partiler* (Istanbul: Hürriyet Vakfi Yayinlari, 1986).

The Contributors

Eva Bellin
Department of Government and the Center for Middle Eastern Studies, Harvard University

Laurie Brand
Department of International Relations, University of Southern California

Sheila Carapico
Department of Political Science, University of Richmond, VA

Jill Crystal
Department of Political Science, Auburn University, GA

Gideon Doron
Department of Political Science, Tel Aviv University

John P. Entelis
Professor of Political Science, Fordham University, NY

Nilüfer Göle
Department of Sociology, Boğaziçi University, Istanbul

Abdelbaki Hermassi
Ambassador of Tunisia to UNESCO, Paris

Neil Hicks
Lawyers Committee for Human Rights, New York City

Raymond A. Hinnebusch
Department of Political Science and International Relations, The College of St. Catherine, MN

Zuhair Humadi
Organization for Human Rights in Iraq

Saad Eddin Ibrahim
Ibn Khaldoun Center for Developmental Studies, Cairo

Farhad Kazemi
Department of Politics, New York University

Ann Mosely Lesch
Department of Political Science, Villanova University, PA

Abdeslam Maghraoui
Middle East Institute, Washington, DC

Antoine Messarra
Department of Political Science, Beirut University

Ahmad Moussalli
Department of Political Science, American University of Beirut

Muhammad Muslih
Department of Political Science, Long Island University

Ghanim al-Najjar
Department of Political Science, University of Kuwait

Augustus Richard Norton
Department of International Relations, Boston University

Atef Odhibat
Department of Political Science, Yarmuk University, Amman

Alan Richards
Department of Economics, University of California, Santa Cruz

Sara Roy
Center for Middle East Studies, Harvard University

Mustapha Kamil al-Sayyid
Department of Political Science, Cairo University

Jillian Schwedler
Department of Politics, New York University

Binnaz Toprak
Department of Political Science and International Relations,
Boğaziçi University, Istanbul

About the Book

In virtually every part of the world, pluralist, participant governments seem to be triumphing over despotism—with the exception of the Middle East. Is the region immune to the global trend toward democracy? Are Middle Easterners content to live under authoritarianism, whether secular or religious? Does the "traditional," Islamic culture of the region simply prohibit the emergence of democracy? The study of civil society in the Middle East illustrates that, for each question, the answer is clearly no.

Across the Middle East, citizens are meeting formally and informally every day to discuss issues ranging from health and social services to economic policy and politics. Some Middle Eastern governments tolerate these gatherings; others strictly forbid and harshly repress them. But while the viability of these organizations remains a contested issue, civil society in the Middle East has emerged as an important topic of debate among scholars, activists, policymakers, and citizens alike.

This book provides both an introduction to the topic and a guide to further readings and resources. The opening chapter surveys the major theoretical debates and contrasts various approaches to the study of civil society in the Middle East. A collection of pithy summaries follow, each highlighting the quality of political life in a Middle Eastern state and evaluating the vitality and significance of its civil society. Three additional overviews address economic liberalization and democracy, Islamist debates concerning civil society and political reform, and government strategies of including or excluding Islamist participants. There is also an extensive bibliography of sources in Arabic, English, French, and Turkish.

Jillian Schwedler served as program officer of the civil Society in the Middle East Project at New York University. Author of several articles on social movements and electoral politics in the contemporary Middle East, she is currently conducting field research for a book examining the participation of Islamist political parties in the 1993 multiparty parliamentary elections in Yemen and Jordan.

124